Praise for The Badass
Black Girl Series

"In an era when Black girls are bombarded with negative stereotypes on traditional and social media platforms, *Badass Black Girl* offers welcome advice to Black girls to embrace their individuality and to develop positive mental and body images. Writing in clear understandable prose, Fievre provides numerous examples of women such as a Toni Morrison, Michelle Obama, and Madam C. J. Walker, who exemplify Black excellence, and equips Black girls through a series of exercises and affirmations with the tools to become 'Badass' women who know their worth."
—Geoffrey Philp, author of *Garvey's Ghost*

"Protecting our young Black women and femme-identifying youth is so important—M.J. Fievre lays this out with grace, care, and the most powerful love in the phenomenal *Badass Black Girl*. So often, our society tells us that we're so strong, so resilient, so able to fix everyone else's world—this book reveals the truth: Black women/femme-identifying people are just as tender, just as in need of affirmation and praise, just as worthy of an embrace from self and from those around us. [*Badass Black Girl*] is a celebration, an affirmation, a history text, a little bit of memoir, and an exuberant prayer for the prosperity of Black women."
—Ashley M. Jones, author of *Magic City Gospel*

"M.J. Fievre gives every girl her own set of black pearls of wisdom."
—Marie Ketsia Theodore-Pharel, author of *Beauty Walks in Nature*

"*Badass Black Girl* is the big hug you need, […] a glorious love letter to the Black women who have shaped and loved us, to our griots and groundbreakers. […] Fievre celebrates Black girls in all of their power, vulnerability, and beauty and offers instructions for self-love, taking responsibility, creating art, and expressing gratitude. I wish I had

[*Badass Black Girl*] when I was younger, and I'm happy I have it now."
—Jennifer Maritza McCauley, author of *SCAR ON/SCAR OFF*

"You'll come away from *Badass Black Girl* feeling as if you've known the author your entire life, and it's a rare feat for any writer. M.J. Fievre is the best friend, the confidante everyone yearns for."
—Michael Reid, "Mike, the Poet," author of *Dear Woman* and *The Boyfriend Book*

"Finding the courage to live as you are is not easy, so *Badass Black Girl* is […] designed to help young girls to nurture their creativity, self-motivation, and positive self-awareness. This is a journal that celebrates girl power and honors the strength and spirit of black girls."
—Mary Cowper, Midwest Book Review

"The world is often unkind to Black girls and Black women. Issues Black women have historically faced—oppression, racism, sexism, economic strife—are sometimes compounded in unimaginable ways. […] The words from influential Black female role models, combined with Fievre's own wisdom regarding self-love and self-esteem, will give readers the feeling of being heard and understood. Fievre's tips for affirmations and other positive strategies are the tools her readers will able to utilize in their lives. It's time for us Black girls and Black women to be empowered, and I'm glad we have Fievre to show us the way."
—Monique Jones, author of *The Book of Awesome Black Americans*

Empowered Black Girl

Joyful Affirmations
& Words of Resilience

M.J. Fievre

mango
PUBLISHING

CORAL GABLES

Cover Design: Elina Diaz
Cover Photo/illustration: Cincinart/stock.adobe.com
Layout & Design: Elina Diaz

For permission requests, please contact the publisher at:
Mango Publishing Group
2850 S Douglas Road, 2nd Floor
Coral Gables, FL 33134 USA
info@mango.bz

For special orders, quantity sales, course adoptions and corporate sales, please email the publisher at sales@mango.bz. For trade and wholesale sales, please contact Ingram Publisher Services at customer.service@ingramcontent.com or +1.800.509.4887.

Empowered Black Girl: Joyful Affirmations & Words of Resilience

Library of Congress Cataloging-in-Publication number: Has been requested
ISBN: (print) 978-1-64250-560-3, (ebook) 978-1-64250-561-0
BISAC category code: YAN006020, YOUNG ADULT NONFICTION / Biography & Autobiography / Cultural, Ethnic & Regional

Printed in the United States of America

Empowered
Black Girl

Table of Contents

INTRODUCTION

"Everybody's talking at me." Most people are stuck listening to competing voices as they go about their daily routine. The nature of public life makes it hard to escape. The news of the world is constantly blaring on television, and everyone has an opinion about something, whether it is the barista who says she needs Botox or the man on the corner who claims the end of the world is coming. Life, with all its noise, can be overwhelming, especially when you consider that you have competing voices within yourself to contend with.

Many of us are like the old cartoon where a lost soul is stuck between a battle of consciences: an angel on one shoulder, whispering how beautiful and remarkable you are, urging you to be good, feel good, behave yourself, and a little devil with a pitchfork on the other shoulder, whispering, "You're no good." This inner critic tells you not to bother, and its voice can become so ingrained in us we forget we don't have to listen to it, and we fall into behaviors we know aren't good for our self-esteem, our health, and our sense of well-being.

If you have been listening to the inner critic for too long, it's time to start letting your wiser voice have the floor. Affirmations are a great way to silence that inner nag and bring positivity into your life. You can think of them as the voice of your angelic conscience. But in order to hear your wise conscience, you have to become more conscious of what you're listening to. Your wise conscience never says, "You're not good enough." Your wise conscience knows full well she is speaking truth when she says, "Look at you! Now you're a badass, for sure."

You hear it all the time: you have to accept yourself as you are. Love your identity. Love your heritage. Be proud!

But how? Do you simply wake up one morning and magically think, *I'm the best thing since sliced bread?*

Do you simply say, "Hey, I love myself?"

Actually, yes.

Well, yes—and no. It starts with the affirmation—*I love myself*—and, little by little, you actually do learn to love every facet of yourself, you learn to *really* believe in yourself. You become this girl you imagine: ambitious, strong, thirsty for more.

Positive affirmations empower you. They are short, simple ("I am happy"), and yet very powerful, and you can use them as a mantra to get what you want—confidence, for instance. They allow you to believe in yourself, to develop high self-esteem, and to turn your thoughts into action.

Affirmations can bring big changes in your life by making things happen for you, but to be effective, an affirmation must be repeated several times, and over several days. The repetitions turn the affirmation into a state of mind—into a conviction. And you know what they say: change your thoughts, change your life.

You can repeat your affirmation in the morning, during your daily routine in the bathroom—while combing your hair or applying your makeup. You can whisper it as you fall asleep, or while you're running in the neighborhood. At first, it might feel a little awkward to talk to yourself in this manner, but part of how affirmations work is that you are convincing yourself of the truth of the statement. You'll notice as you repeat the affirmation that your tone of voice might change from one that is almost questioning the affirmation to one that is declaring an obvious truth boldly.

Think of how you talk to yourself now. What words do you use to talk about yourself?

Too often, we self-sabotage.

"I'm not enough…"
"I do not deserve…"
"I'm afraid of…"
"I am worth less than…"
"I cannot because…"
"I'm not ready yet…"
"I have no chance…"
"It is difficult to…"
"I will never make it…"
"I don't have the strength to…"
"I'm not going to get there."
"I suck."

Self-sabotage is just a waste of time. It leads to pain and suffering. Each negative interaction with yourself pokes the pitchfork a little deeper under your skin, until you begin to believe the horrible things you say to yourself. Things you wouldn't say to your best friend. It's time to silence the inner critic.

You are magic. You always have been.

Now You Can Begin

Affirmation Stations

Throughout the book, I've placed little stopping points for you called "Affirmation Stations." The purpose of having multiple affirmations is so that you can choose one that is calling to you at your present stage of the journey or that just feels right to you.

But you can read multiple affirmations if you are in dire need of a pick me up. Write some of them on little slips of paper and keep them in your pocket for when you need a reminder. Tape them to your refrigerator or bathroom mirror. Write them in your calendar. The more often you remind yourself that you've begun listening to reason, the more you will benefit from having them near. You can open the book randomly and find them, or you can read the book (I highly recommend this) from beginning to end.

Badass to the Bone

Throughout the book you'll also find quotes from badass Black women. All of these women faced the same kind of hardships most of us face, but they made a conscious choice to overcome their obstacles and be bright beacons of hope for others. Use these quotes whenever you need to hear the voice of wise women. In addition to reading them, you can embroider them and frame them, hang them in conspicuous places, or tweet them; whatever you feel will pay homage to the words and bring you closer to the message they convey.

After reading this book, you will have a whole plethora of affirmations to try out. If this is your first time practicing affirmations, you may want to journal about the experience and note how you feel when you start. It's typical to feel a little uncomfortable at first. You may have a hard time saying the words with conviction. Your palms might get a little sweaty. That's all normal. In your journal, you can write down how you feel each time you practice the affirmation. If it doesn't start to get easier, or if it still feels awkward, you may want to try a different affirmation until you find one that fits. You may want to write an affirmation of your own. You'll find that when you start practicing, that nagging inner voice of self-sabotage will start to die away and be replaced with a much kinder voice that has your back. Listen to it. If it says something you need to hear, you can repeat that also.

Try saying your affirmation while looking at yourself in the mirror. Really look directly into your own eyes. Throw your shoulders back, and say the words like you mean them. Then, you can say them to yourself whenever you need a reminder. In no time, you'll feel more confident and secure in your own identity. But you can't just say the affirmations and expect everything is going to change for you. You have to follow up the affirmations with actions. If you say to yourself in the morning, "I am beautiful," make sure you dress in a way that makes you *feel beautiful.* If you tell yourself, "I am a success," then do the things that successful people do. Work hard. Eat right. Get enough sleep.

Becoming more confident and secure will help you get further in life and feel better about yourself. You got this! I believe in you.

CHAPTER ONE

....

Confidence—
Dare to Be Powerful

"I am no longer accepting the things I cannot change. I am changing the things I cannot accept."

—**Dr. Angela Davis**, American political activist, philosopher, academic, and author; she has written about police violence and abuses in the prison system since the 1970s

As a Black girl, you need confidence to assert yourself. When you're confident, it doesn't matter what anyone tells you or tries to make you believe. You look at yourself in the mirror and you think, *I'm amazing.* And when society refuses to give you room to fully exist, you create a well-defined place for yourself. You say: "Enough! I'm not 'less than' anybody. I'm not less attractive. I'm not less intelligent. I'm not less capable." You let your voice be heard when magazines or TV shows or people around you subtly denigrate Black beauty and Black culture—or try to erase Blackness altogether. Because you know better than to believe their message. You know that Blackness is to be celebrated, that the accomplishments of Black girls are to be brought to light and applauded. You won't stand for people putting you down. Nothing will keep you from setting and reaching your goals.

Are you that girl—confident and totally badass?

Maybe not yet. Maybe you're still struggling to find your place in the world. Maybe sometimes being Black feels like a burden, and when you look at yourself, you feel down, or just plain tired of having to talk about your identity, of having to think about the way the world sees you…or doesn't see you. It's possible that you're surrounded by people who assume you'll never amount to anything. And, to be honest, maybe sometimes you wish you were something else— someone else. People might tell you that, from the outside, you seem to have confidence in yourself, but in fact, you feel that you have a lot to work on.

Now you just have to use positive affirmations to activate your #BlackGirlMagic.

As a Black girl, you need four types of affirmations in order to gain confidence:

1. Affirmations that recognize your inner beauty

2. Affirmations that help you embrace your Black body

3. Affirmations that celebrate collective Black identities

4. Affirmations that celebrate your strengths

Recognize Your Inner Beauty

"I'm convinced that we Black women possess a special indestructible strength that allows us to not only get down, but to get up, to get through, and to get over."

—**Janet Jackson**, American singer, songwriter, actress, and dancer who first began performing at the age of seven and has sold over a hundred million records worldwide

This is what the world will have you believe: Being Black is a weight on your shoulders that will drag you down.

Because of the color of your skin, they'll make you think you have less value or that you're less intelligent.

You need to learn to love who you are, not just your complexion, your facial features, and other physical traits that make you unique; you should also celebrate your history, your strong personality, your unique qualities, and the goals you've set for yourself. You need to appreciate the ways in which you're changing, evolving. You are not perfect, of course, but you have the distinction of being unique.

Affirmations Station

+ I am Black and I matter.

+ I am Black. I deserve to be seen and heard.

+ I am Black. I love myself and I accept myself completely.

+ I am Black. I deserve love and respect.

+ I am Black. I have the right, like everyone else, to have the same privileges.

+ I am Black. Day by day, I am more and more confident.

There is no one else quite like you, and that's a gift, so choose to believe in yourself. You are lucky to have your own prisms, your own emotions, your own quirks. Embrace them.

Badass to the Bone

"When I'm not feeling my best, I ask myself, 'What are you gonna do about it?' I use the negativity to fuel the transformation into a better me."

—**Beyoncé**, American singer, songwriter, record producer, dancer, and actress; she has won over twenty-three Grammys, all while building a thriving career and family

"I'll stick to finding the funny in the ordinary because my life is pretty ordinary and so are the lives of my friends—and my friends are hilarious."

—**Issa Rae,** American actress, writer, and producer; starting from YouTube, Rae started an empire and launched a recurring series on HBO

"Believing you are unworthy of love and belonging—that who you are authentically is a sin or is wrong—is deadly. Who you are is beautiful and amazing."

—**Laverne Cox**, American actress, producer, and LGBTQ+ advocate; she started the hashtag #TransIsBeautiful to encourage self-love in trans people who have a hard time accepting their true selves

"The voice of a Black woman should always be HERSELF."

—**Malebo Sephodi**, writer, activist, development worker, and social commentator; she wrote a book to spark conversation on what it looks like to "misbehave" and go against the patriarchy

"Even if it makes others comfortable, I will LOVE who I am."

—**Janelle Monáe**, American singer, songwriter, rapper, actress, and producer; an advocate for Black, feminist, and queer identities, her intersectionality is apparent in her music, her fashion, and her activism

"Just be yourself, it's the easiest thing to be. Black girls, we just on another level."

—**Rihanna**, Barbadian singer, songwriter, actress, businesswoman, and philanthropist; she successfully launched her own line of affordable makeup to help solve diversity issues in the cosmetic and skincare industry

"I think there is room to be our entire selves. There is room to be joyous and funny and still be taken seriously."

—**Mahogany Browne**, American poet and author; she coordinated the Women of the World poetry slam series to highlight the voices of women

"Self-love has very little to do with how you feel about your outer self. It's about accepting all of yourself."

—**Tyra Banks**, model and businesswoman; she was the first African American woman to be featured in *Sports Illustrated* magazine

Embrace Your Black Body

"Dipped in chocolate, bronzed in elegance, enameled with grace, toasted with beauty. My Lord, she's a Black woman."

—**Dr. Yosef Ben-Jochannan**, American writer and historian

We cannot change the standards of beauty that other people hold—but we can define our own. Look at yourself with new eyes, admire your beauty, and accept it! Change your idea of what a perfect body looks like. Who cares if you have hyperpigmentation, for example, and so what if others can see that your body has different tones when you wear a swimsuit? Your body is a miracle! How beautiful it is to contain you.

Maybe people around you don't understand how you can be a Black girl and not have curves in all the right places, and maybe your breasts aren't as voluptuous as the women's in magazines. It's possible that you still haven't come to love your natural hair, your face without makeup, without artifice. It is important to build yourself up and to realize that, as a Black girl, you must learn to love your Black skin, your Black shapes, your Black hair.

Instead of obsessing about whether your body is desirable to other people, wear it with pride and celebrate its differences.

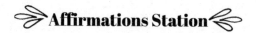

Affirmations Station

Some of the affirmations you can use to embrace your Black body:

+ My body is soft, smooth, and rich.

+ My voice is soft as honey, but my tone is powerful and wild like fire.

+ My Black body is a beautiful vessel in all that it is and all that it is becoming.

+ This body, my body, has a skin that shelters it with strength.

+ I wear my Black body with pride.

+ Black health matters. My health matters.

Look long and hard at your body, and accept that this is the only one you will get. Acknowledge the strength and vitality of your Black body. Notice how each part of you takes up physical space, and tell yourself that your body is worthy of taking up space. *Let it* take up space, and then more space, and even more space. Reclaim what is rightfully yours: the right to move freely, to live, and be joyful.

Badass to the Bone

"I'm a Black woman every day and I'm not confused about that. I'm not worried about that. I don't need to have a discussion with you about how I feel as a Black woman, because I don't feel disempowered as a Black woman."

—**Shonda Rhimes**, American author and writer-producer for TV and film; she was the first African American female to serve as executive producer for a broadcast network

"I consider myself a crayon. I might not be your favorite color, but one day you're going to need me to complete your picture."

—**Lauryn Hill**, American singer, songwriter, and rapper; she was the first woman to win five Grammys in one year

"I am not tragically colored. There is no great sorrow dammed up in my soul, nor lurking behind my eyes… Even in the helter-skelter skirmish that is my life, I have seen that the world is to the strong regardless of a little pigmentation more or less. No, I do not weep at the world—I am too busy sharpening my oyster knife."

—**Zora Neale Hurston**, American author, anthropologist, and filmmaker; she had to fight for her education, receiving her high school diploma at twenty-six and her bachelor's degree at thirty-seven

"I used to think I was ugly. I thought I looked like a camel. A person who doesn't love themselves, they will see anything that pops up on their face. I've seen squirrels, I've seen a bird, and I've seen all kinds of animals on my face. But that is the result of self-hate. I've learned to say: 'You know what? I am a beautiful Black woman.'"

—**Mary J. Blige**, American singer-songwriter, actress, and philanthropist; she dropped out of high school when a karaoke recording of her singing reached Uptown Records; she went on to win nine Grammy awards

"I think any Black woman is a queen. It's just, do you know it? Do you see it in yourself? Do you recognize it, do you abide by that, do you define yourself as that? Based on who we are and what we've been through and how we survive and where we stand, we are on kind of sacred ground. We stand on the backs of our ancestors."

—**Ava DuVernay**, American writer, producer, director, and distributor of independent films; she is adamant about shattering the glass ceiling of the entertainment industry one film at a time

"I'm an Exquisite Black Queen! I like, love, and celebrate myself. I don't fit society's beauty standards, but I'm beautiful to me. I know my worth and I respect who I am as a woman. I've got beauty on the inside and that makes me empowered and powerful. I'm fearless and comfortable in my own skin. I've got flaws, but I'm still confident! This Queen right here is flawed yet phenomenal, valuable, and unique!"

—**Stephanie Lahart**, poet, author, and empowerment writer; she's written books to encourage and uplift women to know and love themselves

"I am a Black woman. The music of my song, some sweet arpeggio of tears, is written in a minor key and I can be heard humming in the night."

—**Mari Evans**, African American poet, writer, and dramatist associated with the Black Arts Movement; she created *The Black Experience*, a TV show that interviewed and showcased Black luminaries

"How do you keep the Black female body present, and how do you own value for something that society won't give value to? It's a question I try to answer through my own life."

—**Claudia Rankine**, American poet, essayist, and playwright; she is the author of five volumes of poetry, two plays, and various essays

"And I think about all the things we could be if we were never told our bodies were not built for them."

—**Elizabeth Acevedo**, Afro-Dominican American poet; she won a Carnegie Medal for her book *The Poet X*

"The ancients walk within us."

—**M. NourbeSe Philip**, poet and writer; she left a promising career as a lawyer to write full time

Celebrate Collective Black Identity

"Black girl magic is a rallying call of recognition. Embedded in the everyday is a magnificence that is so easy to miss because we're so mired in the struggle and what society says we are."

—**Ava DuVernay**, American writer, producer, director, and distributor of independent films

Your own life was birthed from a history of defiance, courage, and determination not to succumb to oppression. Think way back, thousands of years, to powerful queens like Nefertiti and Cleopatra, who ruled in Egypt. Those are your foremothers, even if they don't share a bloodline with you. They are part of a history that led you to where you are today as a young woman in the world. Now think back just over a hundred and fifty years ago, right here in America, to foremothers like Harriet Tubman, born into slavery, who along with her Underground Railroad workers smuggled enslaved people across the Mason-Dixon line to freedom. Nobody stopped her. Think of Sojourner Truth, another fugitive from slavery, who in 1851, at a women's rights convention, tore off her shirt and asked the men gathered around, sneering at her, "Ain't I a woman?" She asked that question because being a woman means something powerful. It has always been a powerful thing to be a woman, even when our rights were stripped from us.

Millions of strong Black women have lived and died since Tubman and Truth, and we build on their legacies one life at a time. It is your time to build a legacy for tomorrow that others will look back on and remember. It can be as big or as small as you will it to be, but it's all part of a collective legacy that will get passed to the children who come after you. We are all part of a global village. We all have a piece of the future within our command. How dare you ever be ashamed of who you are—of where you came from? Celebrate your heritage. Your ancestry. It's powerful.

Do you know your story? Where were you born? Why were you given the name you have? What do you know about your parents and about their parents? What legacy have they built for you? You will not be taught this kind of history at school. There is so much history for you to learn that doesn't make it into your textbooks. And, of course, there is the internet. But most importantly there's your family, who can answer many of your questions. It's up to you to take the initiative, research your story, and learn more about your identity. Understanding where you came from will help you see the direction you want your life to take, and it can be any direction you choose for yourself.

Knowledge will be a bridge that will connect you to your origins.

Affirmations Station

+ I am Black and I am proud of my identity.

+ I keep my self-control around people who question my history and my identity.

+ I protect myself from people who question my values and my culture.

+ I realize with wisdom and discernment the discrimination that my community encounters.

+ I forgive myself for feeling anger, hatred, or contempt for people who see me as an inferior being.

+ The strength of my ancestors is so bright that it becomes more than enough.

Badass to the Bone

"Black Girl Magic means that I have the power to overcome anything. Especially when we're in a world where you're told that you can't do something or you're less than, I'm reminded that my ancestors have overcome so much. There's still so much work to be done, and I have the power to overcome it."

—**Michelle Carter**, Gold medalist Olympian; she has been to three Olympics, beating her own shot-putting record, and has held her high school's record since 2003

"My Blackness does not inhibit me from being beautiful and intelligent. In fact, it is the reason I am beautiful and intelligent. And you cannot stop me."

—**Amandla Stenberg**, American actress and singer; she uses her platform to help teens cope with anxiety and to call out multibillionaires for cultural appropriation

"I say 'magic' because it's something that people don't always understand. Sometimes our accomplishments might seem to come out of thin air, because a lot of times, the only people supporting us are other Black women."

—**CaShawn Thompson**, creator of #BlackGirlMagic; she built her brand at the age of forty, without a degree, to encourage beauty and strength in Black and brown girls

"I am a product of every other Black woman before me who has done or said anything worthwhile. Recognizing that I am part of history is what allows me to soar."

—**Oprah Winfrey**, American talk show host, actress, television producer, media executive, and philanthropist; she uses her platforms to lift other talented and creative Black writers to the forefront

"I can't believe my good fortune. I'm so grateful to be a Black woman. I would be so jealous if I were anything else."

—**Maya Angelou**, American poet, memoirist, and civil rights activist; a sexual assault left her mute when she was young, until a teacher helped her to read and speak again

"Black girls rock because they can't help themselves."

—**Iyanla Vanzant**, American inspirational speaker, lawyer, spiritual teacher, author, life coach, and television personality; she shares her stories to encourage women to live a life of spiritual and mental freedom

"God made me this way, so I have to be happy with who I am. And it's a journey. And I embrace my brown-skin sisters. I love them and I hope that they embrace me."

—**Kym Whitley**, American comedian and actress; she adopted the abandoned baby of a young woman she was mentoring

"Be comfortable in your Black skin. If someone finds a threat in it, then they should visit their psychologist."

—**Mitta Xinindlu**, South African writer and researcher whose work focuses on social justice issues; she knows ten languages and is 100 percent fluent in three

Celebrate Your Strengths

"You've got to get in the fight. It is time to take off the handcuffs. It's time to get in it."

—**Maxine Waters**, American congresswoman; the first female African American chair of the House Financial Services Committee, she's notorious for making waves all throughout her political career

"I have learned over the years that when one's mind is made up, this diminishes fear; knowing what must be done does away with fear."

—**Rosa Parks**, American activist; known for her pivotal role in the Montgomery bus boycott, she's the first Black woman to have a statue in the US Capitol

"I'm really not one about reform, I'm about tearing it down, revolution."

—**Aja Monet**, poet, writer, activist, and educator; she's the youngest woman to win the Nuyorican Poets Cafe Grand Slam title and uses her voice to speak against police brutality

Being proud to be Black can be difficult when you talk about your ambitions…and someone glances at you in a way that says it all: "But you know you are Black, right? There is no way you can get there." "You're so ghetto," they say. "You're low class; you're loud… Your name is stupid. You're not going anywhere."

Don't conform to what others say you are—or should be. Don't wait for validation from others: you have nothing to prove! The way you feel about yourself should not depend on the ways other people feel about you. Black people have a powerful history, filled with trailblazers and innovators whose work pushed boundaries in the fields of science, technology, engineering, art, and medicine and are role models with creative, innovative, and life-affirming genius.

You don't need to be appreciated by *everyone*. Turn down the noise! Be selective and surround yourself with positivity as much as you can. Get information and advice from the right people—those who soothe you, challenge you, reassure you, the ones that ultimately bring you what you need when you need it. As long as you take care to water your interior garden and strive to trust your inner voice and your instincts, you will see the confidence you carry revealed soon enough.

Choose a role model. Sometimes we just need to identify with someone, learn from their journey, their choices, their vision, and admire their success. This will bring you confidence and a sense of pride. There are so many: Maya Angelou, Naomi Campbell, Oprah Winfrey, Beyoncé… And this person does not need to be a celebrity to inspire you… It can be a person around you: your mother, your sister, your friend… It may be that your role model is someone who has been a trailblazer in their field, someone you look up to and want to emulate, or someone whose work you want to continue. Know that you can also be a model for others and have an impact on their worlds.

Positivity attracts positivity. So avoid anything that generates negativity and anxiety in your life—situations that make you uncomfortable, toxic people around you—and you'll see how much easier it'll be to sharpen your skills. Create an environment that inspires you, soothes you, excites you, and gives you the opportunity to gain self-confidence. You will see that by staying in a cocoon full of positivity, your confidence will eventually find a place in you and will reveal itself. The answers you are looking for, for the most part, are already within you.

Affirmations Station

+ I have confidence in myself, in my Black girl magic, and in my unconditionally loving heart.

+ I have the courage to realize my dreams; I dare to try and I'm proud of it.

+ I was born to succeed; I am capable of extraordinary things.

+ I have everything I need to succeed, and I am determined to reach my goals.

+ I give myself permission to step out of my role as a victim and take more responsibility for my life.

+ The past is gone, now I have control of my life and I move on.

Badass to the Bone

"Be true to your convictions, and do not settle. You may take some detours and encounter some roadblocks along the way, but never give up on the pursuit of excellence—however you may define that for yourself."

—**Elaine Welteroth**, American journalist, editor, and author; she shook up *Teen Vogue* by infusing a politically and socially aware consciousness into the pages of the magazine

"I didn't learn to be quiet when I had an opinion. The reason they knew who I was is because I told them."

—**Ursula Burns**, American businesswoman; she was the first African American woman to serve as CEO of a Fortune 500 company

"I am very strong and very opinionated. My 'no' means 'no,' my 'yes' means 'yes.' I'm not negotiating certain things. I don't feel like I have to become something I'm not."

—**Beyoncé**, American singer, songwriter, record producer, dancer, and actress

"When I dare to be powerful—to use my strength in the service of my vision, then it becomes less and less important whether I am afraid."

—**Audre Lorde**, American author and activist; she wrote on the struggles of being Black, being a woman, and being a lesbian

"I have standards I don't plan on lowering for anybody…including myself."

—**Zendaya**, American actress and singer; for her eighteenth birthday she campaigned to feed impoverished children, and for her twentieth raised $50,000 to support a women's empowerment initiative

"As a Black woman, I have no particular interest in maintaining the status quo. Why would I? The status quo is harmful; the status quo is significantly racist and sexist and a whole bunch of other things that I think need to change."

—**N. K. Jemisin**, American science fiction and fantasy writer; she wrote a trilogy while working full-time that went on to win her three Hugo Best Novel awards

"I definitely am drawn to strong females who are successful, smart women because I am a woman like that."

—**Megalyn Echikunwoke**, American actress; she was raised on a Navajo reservation in Chinle, Arizona, with her brother and sister

"As an actress, I have put myself out there as an independent Black woman, a single mom, a go-getter, a hustler who isn't afraid to survive."

—**LisaRaye McCoy-Misick**, American actress, model, businesswoman, and fashion designer; she describes herself as knowing when to fold and when to hold

You are only a tiny twig in the uppermost branches of a great tree that has been growing for eons. At your roots are the roots of civilization and powerful, brave foremothers. When you look in the mirror, be proud of not just your own beauty but the beauty of the whole tree that grew before you. Stand up straight, and be bold and caring. It takes courage to be someone you can be proud of. Embrace the magic of being Black and beautiful in a world that turns its eyes away sometimes, and be different by pointing out the beauty you see in the world and reflecting it in yourself.

CHAPTER TWO

....

What's LOVE Got to Do with It?

Love is the key to a better world, but making the choice to love others can be the hardest thing to do in life. Why should you care about someone else's well-being, let alone their happiness, when as a Black girl your own life is so darn complex and often brings a lot of daily pressures? It took you so long to get to a place where you're confident and accepting of yourself. It took so much work to acknowledge that you're a *queen*. Shouldn't it be all about you now? Ugh. Should you even bother with those folks who won't even try to understand the difference between "Black lives matter," "Black lives *also* matter," and "All lives matter"?

Is there really a point in being selfless, in getting involved in causes that have nothing to do with you? There is. "Every man must decide whether he will walk in the light of creative altruism or in the light of destructive selfishness," according to Dr. Martin Luther King.

Without love you cannot change the world. "Always remember, you have within you the strength, the patience, and the passion to reach for the stars to change the world," says Harriet Tubman.

Be aware. You have your own problems, your own fears and insecurities, and you always have to take care of yourself first. You have to find a balance between taking care of *you*—and taking care of others. For example, if you were starving, you would have to feed yourself before you could feed anyone else. But if you have enough, why not share? Besides, life can get busy. It's important not to get lost in the spiral of things happening—it will keep you from being aware of the world and its difficulties: only when you're fully in sync with the world around you can you improve it, and, at the same time, breathe new meaning into other people's lives and into your own. Your actions have a much longer lifespan than you might think: they live in the short, medium and long term. A selfish action that is repeated every day in the short term will ultimately have a long-term consequence. Don't be indifferent to other people—work for a better world!

Listen. Love starts with listening to what people have to say and getting to know them. *Actually* listen. Don't just pretend to listen while thinking about something else. Give others the opportunity to express themselves, to share their worries or an exciting story—even if you don't like it. If you tend to monopolize the conversation, you'll be unable to know how others feel. By being constantly concerned about your own problems and your own ideas, you will have neither the time nor the energy to be selfless.

Keep your feelings in check. Indifference or even cruelty have no place among altruists. Enjoy seeing others happy. As you find your own happiness in the happiness of others, you are more likely to seek out more ways to be selfless. Be positive and kind. Becoming selfless is impossible without positivity! Avoid being pessimistic or fatalistic; it keeps you from giving to others. Positivity is essential in understanding others; kindness also goes hand in hand with understanding and will give you the ability to forgive and move on. Get rid of negative assumptions, and choose instead neutrality, diplomacy—or passion!

Empathize. Be sensitive both to the joys but also to the sorrows of those around you. Being selfless involves being able to see past your personal issues and be empathetic, even to people you've never met. Empathy and altruism are inseparable. If you understand someone else's feelings, you will be more likely to show altruism toward that person. You could also develop empathy for people you've never met. Practice putting yourself in someone else's shoes. If you were faced with their problems, how would you feel? How would you like to be treated? When you have a lot of empathy, you easily put yourself in the place of the other, you more easily feel what they feel, and you share your emotions. Compassion is an innate feeling in response to the suffering of the other, it is a deep reaction that comes from the heart. The more empathy we have, the more we are able to feel compassion.

Show solidarity. While everything might be going right for you, this might not necessarily be the case for those around you. Make it your moral duty to live in solidarity with others. If you know someone close to you is going through a difficult time, find out how you can best support them. Cultivate a desire to help others by asking them, for example, how you could make yourself useful to them.

Act selflessly. Helping without expecting anything in return is not an easy task. We live in a society that rewards good deeds—with recognition, for example. Acting selflessly requires a little training: you can start by making an anonymous and generous donation to an association, for instance. You'll get nothing in return except the happiness of having been able to help. Be altruistic, even when no one realizes you're doing it. Have you ever felt a thrill of happiness in making someone happy? Some people wonder if it is possible to be genuinely selfless, since selfless acts can actually create a lot of pleasure. That good feeling you get when you do something selfless is a signal that you're doing something right. Doing kind things is supposed to feel good. Think of how you feel when you do something cruel. You probably feel a little sick and sad inside. That's your body telling you that your actions are harmful. But rather than focusing on whether selflessness isn't actually selfishness, learn to appreciate the happiness of helping others. Altruistic people do not act with kindness and generosity because they're waiting for their merit to be recognized. They do it because it is the right thing to do, and because they are happy to be able to help others when they can.

Think globally. Focus on the common good. Altruism is a veritable crusade against individualism, so it is logical to try to establish mutual support, a group dynamic. Meditate. Seeing beyond your personal problems is no easy task. But to get there, it is important to give yourself time to meditate. Giving yourself this time for reflection will allow you to refocus on what's essential.

Being altruistic means doing good around you on a regular basis in a selfless way, without looking for your own interest. Here are some ideas for how to be altruistic on a daily basis and make the happiness of others the most direct path to your own happiness (it doesn't have to be a grand gesture):

+ **Become a sponsor.** Donate to a humanitarian organization that works for a cause that is dear to your heart, maybe children's rights or women's rights. Commit to donating even just a few dollars per month to this association. Or volunteer your time. Even a few hours a month can be beneficial.

+ **Practice compassion meditation**. It will increase your propensity to be selfless. To do this, just find a quiet place where you can be alone, relax, sit up straight, and visualize the following: Imagine a mother taking care of her sick child. Share her emotion, her fears, her desire for another being (the child) to regain happiness. Let this feeling grow in you.

+ **Put yourself in other people's shoes.** One of your friends might have made an unpleasant comment about you or might have annoyed you for one reason or another. Well, just put yourself in her shoes. Try to feel what she is going through, her emotions, everything that explains the behavior that initially annoyed you. There is a saying, "You can't understand until you walk a mile in someone else's shoes." We tend to forget sometimes that not everyone is the same—others have their own way of living, of doing, of being. The surest way of learning to love someone is to understand them, so seek to accept others for who they are and where they are in their journey.

✦ **Make an anonymous donation!** Your kindness doesn't have—shouldn't have—to be noticed. That's what makes your selfless act, well, selfless. What about slipping a ten-dollar bill into an envelope that reads, "This is an anonymous gift, have a nice day!" Leave the envelope in a prominent place, where it will not end up in a trash can.

✦ **Give up your spot.** If you are in line, and you find that the person behind you is getting impatient, rather than becoming annoyed, offer them your spot. Even if they refuse, your offer might bring a change in attitude.

✦ **Pay compliments.** When you say nice things to other people, you will feel better, the other person will feel better, and there is a good chance that their attitude will become more positive, which will in turn affect others'. In short, everyone is happy!

✦ **Leave love notes.** Write "You are wonderful" on a Post-it note, and stick it on the bathroom mirror at home, in a cafe, or any other public place. I love this one; when I imagine myself doing it, it makes me particularly happy. You could also write a sweet word on a small piece of paper, and put it either in someone's pocket, in their bag, or under their pillow.

✦ **Care for the homeless.** Offer to buy a homeless person something at the bakery, and ask them what they prefer.

✦ **Offer to help at home**—with meal preparation and the dishes, with babysitting a younger sibling. Give your parents some time to rest. Bake a cake, a pie, pancakes, and treat your parents to breakfast in bed.

✦ **Shower your grandparents with love.** Send a little surprise to your grandparents by mail, even, and especially, if it's not their birthday or another special occasion. Send them drawings or pictures. Give them a phone call! They'll be so happy.

✦ **Be altruistic on the street**. Offer help to someone who seems to be in trouble on the street. This could consist of carrying the groceries of an elderly person, helping a tourist to find his way, helping a person to get on the bus or a disabled person to cross the street.

✦ **Journal.** The power of words is amazing. When I write in my journal about selflessness and loving other people, I feel much lighter and more joyful after. Keep a journal that includes your thoughts about kind actions toward others.

Affirmations Station

Affirmations adapted from the words of Shirley Chisholm, Dorothy Height, Mary McLeod Bethune, Oprah Winfrey, Marian Wright Edelman, and Mae Jemison.

✦ I am, was, and always will be a catalyst for change.

✦ I use myself and anything I can touch to work for justice and freedom.

✦ I invest in the human soul because it's a diamond in the rough.

✦ I lift other people higher.

✦ I don't rain on other people's dreams.

+ I define myself for myself, so I won't be crunched into other people's fantasies for me and eaten alive.

+ I use my imagination, creativity, and curiosity to make the world a better place.

Find a role model. Being selfless is not always pleasant. Putting the needs of others before your own needs is usually worth it, but it can be extremely difficult at times to act in the interests of someone else when you too have needs to meet. To do this, follow the example of selfless people you admire to help you make the right choices. There are so many powerful, strong Black women for you to emulate. Don't just look for famous people to admire. Admire the single mother with three kids who works a full-time job too. When you can see how hard it is to be remarkable, you gain a better understanding of what it takes to change the world. Remember, you're already remarkable. It's just difficult sometimes.

Badass to the Bone

"The more I wonder, the more I love."

—**Alice Walker**, American novelist, poet, and social activist; once sent to jail for trespassing on a naval station, Alice led her fellow prisoners in song

"That's what love did. It came down on you like rain or sunshine."

—**Ntozake Shange,** American playwright, poet, and feminist; her most notable piece, *For Colored Girls Who Have Considered Suicide/When the Rainbow Is Enuf,* had a two-year run on Broadway

"This was love: a string of coincidences that gathered significance and became miracles."

—**Chimamanda Ngozi Adichie**, Nigerian writer; she began writing at the age of seven, focusing her work on white people until she later found the power in sharing Black stories

"The sweetest joy, the wildest woe, is love."

—**Pearl Bailey**, American actress, humorist, and singer; she received her degree in theology at the age of sixty-seven, proving it's never too late to go after what you want

"Without love, a woman's heart hardens. It becomes a desolate savanna where only cacti grow."

—**Maryse Condé,** Guadeloupean novelist, critic, and playwright; her work explores cultural, racial, and gender issues throughout history, and her novels have been translated into over seven different languages

"In her obvious capacity for love, redemptive and forgiving love, she was alive and standing on the highest peaks of her time and human personality."

—**Margaret Walker**, American poet and writer; she took thirty years to write her novel *Jubilee*, the story of a biracial enslaved women during the American Civil War

"Love is so powerful, it's like unseen flowers under your feet as you walk."

—**Bessie Head**, Motswana writer; her novels focus on the lives of ordinary citizens in post-colonial Africa

"May your hands be an extension of your heart and may you do the work of love with them."

—**Aja Monet**, poet, writer, activist, and educator

Practice Self-Love

Being selfless and carrying out good deeds in the service of others is the surest way to be perfectly happy. Indeed, by performing many good deeds in the service of others, we increase social contacts that have a direct positive impact on our own well-being. Be careful, however: many definitions of altruism associate it with self-denial, putting the needs of others before one's own. But being altruistic doesn't mean focusing all of your attention on others and not caring about yourself. On the contrary, before taking good care of others, and working for their happiness, you must first have knowledge of yourself and treat yourself with a lot of kindness. So if this motivates you more, show a little selfishness to cultivate empathy, compassion, and altruism in yourself, and be happier.

Affirmations Station

Affirmations adapted from words by Wilma Rudolph, Dr. Mae Jemison, and Audre Lorde.

+ I believe in love more than anything in this world.

+ I follow my heart and don't let anybody crush my dreams.

+ I'm not limited by other people's limited imaginations.

+ Every time I love, I love as deeply as if it were forever.

+ I get out there and make it happen for myself and for others.

+ I recognize my right to my thoughts and feelings. I also recognize that others' feelings are valid.

Badass to the Bone

"Always be concerned when a naked man offers you his shirt; a person can't love you if he or she can't love him- or herself."

—**Maya Angelou**, American poet, memoirist, and civil rights activist

"You've got to have something to eat and a little love in your life before you can hold still for any damn body's sermon on how to behave."

—**Billie Holiday**, American jazz and swing singer; while touring with an all-white band, Billie chose to leave when white patrons kept insisting she use the service elevator

"i found god in myself & i loved her i loved her fiercely"

—**Ntozake Shange,** American playwright, poet, and feminist

"I am a feminist, and what that means to me is much the same as the meaning of the fact that I am Black; it means that I must undertake to love myself and to respect myself as though my very life depends upon self-love and self-respect."

—**June Jordan**, Jamaican-American poet, essayist, teacher, and activist; she refused to deny her sexuality and wrote prominently on race, class, sexuality, and political activism

"You've got to learn to leave the table when love's no longer being served."

—**Nina Simone**, American singer, songwriter, musician, and civil rights activist; after the Alabama church bombing, she used her music to protest in a way that couldn't be ignored

"It's all about falling in love with yourself and sharing that love with someone who appreciates you, rather than looking for love to compensate for a self-love deficit."

—**Eartha Kitt**, American singer, actress, dancer, comedian, activist, and author; she once made the wife of then president Lyndon Johnson cry listening to her discuss the Vietnam War

"I guess what everyone wants more than anything else is to be loved."

—**Ella Fitzgerald**, American jazz singer; not considered beautiful by the standards of the 1930s, she used her voice to warm the hearts of all she met

"There is always something left to love. And if you ain't learned that, you ain't learned nothing."

—**Lorraine Hansberry**, American playwright and writer; the first African American female author to have a play performed on Broadway, she fought against unlawful evictions and for gay rights

More about Self-Love

Personal worth does not depend on what we have or what we achieve; it is more to be found in the attitude with which we face every step we take in life, so as to love ourselves unconditionally. It is impossible to give what we do not have. If you do not love yourself, you will find it difficult to love others. You may fall under the illusion of loving other people, but you will inevitably discover that you have descended into manipulation, inordinate demands, and emotional blackmail. When we have not learned to love ourselves unconditionally, we seek that love outside of ourselves, that is, in the people around us. The value we give ourselves will therefore depend on how others perceive and value us. This scenario makes us totally dependent on external evaluation. This type of addiction is extremely damaging, as it can cause us to "beg" for love and tenderness. Indeed, we try to be the center of attention.

"I need to see my own beauty and to continue to be reminded that I am enough, that I am worthy of love without effort, that I am beautiful, that the texture of my hair and that the shape of my curves, the size of my lips, the color of my skin, and the feelings that I have are all worthy and okay."

—**Tracee Ellis Ross**, American actress, singer, and television host; she brings Black women and families into the national spotlight with her acting

You might need more self-love if you:

+ Are withdrawn and/or constantly stressed out

+ Are hypercritical of yourself and/or others

+ Are brusque with others

+ Feel untrustworthy

+ Experience lots of self-doubt

+ Worry more about failures than you celebrate accomplishments

+ Only follow, never lead

+ Feel unloved and unlovable

Integrating mutual care into our lives allows us to meet our own needs, without prioritizing those of others. This allows us to have a global vision in which our desires and those of others coexist in harmony. This is called learning to take care of yourself. Seek out people who can care for you as much as you love them and foster those relationships, because they will sustain you and encourage you to love yourself more.

Take care of yourself. Does your sense of personal worth depend on outside factors? In our culture, it is very common to give too much importance to everything that is external, to everything that happens around us, and loving ourselves is often seen as a selfish act. However, this is a totally mistaken belief, because loving others necessarily begins with loving yourself. Learn to take care of yourself and listen to your own needs.

Accept yourself. It is an act of compassion. Accepting what we are means accepting our faults and discovering our weaknesses, our limits, our abilities, our virtues, and all the things that make us who we are. Greater self-awareness implies greater understanding. When we take care of ourselves, and take the time to understand ourselves, we are able to refrain from judging ourselves and blaming ourselves for the mistakes we have made. In this way, we take the path to accepting ourselves. Through acceptance, we come closer to unconditional love as an act of compassion and to an understanding of who we are, without our own demands limiting our ability to love ourselves and others. By continuing on this path, we will be able to establish relationships that are not based on the search for recognition. By loving each other, we will acquire the power to love those around us in a compassionate way, through acceptance.

Attract Positivity. The more positive your energy is toward others, the more you will attract positive people to you. Energy is very contagious. You can attract toxic and negative people, just like you can attract happy and positive people. It all depends on you and the choices you make in your daily life. Have you noticed that there are certain people around you who are loved by everyone? Know that by doing simple things like helping people, being a positive person, smiling, and being flexible, you increase the amount of love in your life and attract people who want to spend time with you because they enjoy your company.

Affirmations Station

Affirmations adapted from the words of June Jordan, bell hooks, Janelle Monáe, and Audre Lorde.

+ I love myself and respect myself as though my very life depends upon self-love and self-respect.

+ I love myself, and this enables me to deal with whatever life puts before me.

+ I love who I am even if it makes others uncomfortable.

+ I trust myself, and I trust others. I think for myself, I act for myself, I speak for myself—and I encourage others to do the same.

+ I learn to live in harmony with my contradictions, and that keeps me afloat.

+ I live my life fearlessly and encourage others to do the same.

Badass to the Bone

Dr. Maya Angelou was born April 4, 1928, in St. Louis, Missouri. Her parents divorced when she was still young. At the age of eight, Maya was raped by her mother's boyfriend. When she told her brother what had happened to her, her rapist was murdered. This led to a period of several years when Angelou didn't speak. Her book *I Know Why the Caged Bird Sings*, which recounts the sexual assault and its aftermath, was a bestseller and earned international acclaim, even while it was banned in schools for sexual content. Dr. Angelou went on to write thirty-six books. She was a stage performer, singer, dancer, single mother, sex worker, international reporter, inaugural poet, and noted civil rights activist who championed education and Black beauty throughout her life.

"Love liberates. It doesn't just hold—that's ego—love liberates!"

"First best is falling in love. Second best is being in love. Least best is falling out of love. But any of it is better than never having been in love."

"I commend lovers, I am enheartened by lovers, I am encouraged by their courage and inspired by their passion."

"I am grateful that love exists: familial love (love between relatives), romantic love (a passion between lovers), agape love (divine love between God and friends), love of nature (the majesty of mountains, the lasting love of oceans), and the joy of laughter. We are stronger, kinder, and more generous because we live in an atmosphere where love exists."

"I am truly grateful: for being here, for being able to think, for being able to see, for being able to taste, for appreciating love—for knowing that it exists in a world so rife with vulgarity, with brutality and violence… And I'm grateful to know it exists in me, and I'm able to share it with so many people."

"If you find it in your heart to care for somebody else, you will have succeeded."

When Loving Others Is Hard

We can love people who don't like us or who don't show it to us. This is true love! To love someone despite the fact that it is not always reciprocal. However, if this love is one-sided, respect the other's choice not to love you, and respect yourself by choosing the relationship you want with this person. Occasionally, the most loving thing you can do for another person is to let them go and cut off contact with them. You can still love them by wishing them well, but recognize that continuing a relationship with anyone who has toxic habits or is abusive is not being loving toward yourself.

What is "loving the other"?

+ Accepting both their qualities and their flaws.

+ Not judging them for their differences—in culture, in values.

+ Not awaiting recognition.

+ Knowing and respecting them.

Do not judge. We have gotten into the habit of judging, analyzing, gauging others, and it is a very bad habit: Who am I to judge anyone? Do I have all the pieces of their puzzle in my hand? All their history? The ins and outs of their life? Can I make an objective judgment about another person without that knowledge? Of course not. So let's stop judging at all costs, or else let's be judged! Do we like to be judged? Of course not. We would all like to have people who look at us with love, friendship, empathy, and understanding. So let's do it for others! Personally, I remember that each person is in search of love and empathy, and that each human being is capable of the best, but that they simply have not yet expressed it. Each person has inside of themselves holiness, goodness, and love, often well hidden. So let's look for the light in others and love it. When I speak to someone, I remember that deep down, they are a good person. More prosaically, you can also tell yourself that each person is like you, a being alone in the world (one is always alone with oneself), in search of happiness. It's up to you to help them find it! You'll find that you have also found happiness. If you practice this, your life will be transformed. Try it!

Commit to seeing the best in everyone. You can also practice seeing only the good in a person. Basically, this is what we do when we are in love: we romanticize a being and only see their positive sides, those that we like. It is only weeks, months or years later that we also see their flaws. It's up to us to make a practice of seeing only the good qualities and the positive in a person. Sometimes that's not possible. If someone is intent on hurting you, it's okay to walk away. Remember, you do not have to be abused by anyone, ever. But most of the time it is possible to overlook minor flaws and focus on the good qualities a person possesses.

Breathe. If you find it too difficult to see only the good qualities in someone, to refrain from judging them, you can focus on your breathing. You have the *choice* whether or not to get aggravated by what they say and do and the power to detach yourself from them. Look at them as if you were on the bank of a stream watching it flow. This allows you to stop dwelling on your negative thoughts and to have a neutral and benevolent attitude toward others. Love is a feeling that comes from the thoughts you choose to follow or not.

Remember to walk in love. One of the most important things I have learned is the selfless aspect of true love. I'll tell you what it is. Your ability to walk in love each day is more important than anything else. Your "walk in love," is the way you love others and yourself. Selfless love is characterized by the desire to sacrifice one's own desires for those of others. I've learned that authentic love always adapts to the needs and wants of others. Soften your heart, and you'll gradually learn to consider the needs of others. You'll acquire compassion—the sincere desire to put the needs of others before your own. I gradually developed my own "walk in love," making the deliberate decision to reach out to others. I have learned to express my love in different ways to different people. Not everyone has the same needs. One of your parents, for example, may require you to spend more time with them than the other. One friend might need encouragement more often than another.

Spend time with those who are different. (Re)learn to love others. It's important to spend time with those we don't always agree with. Otherwise we end up telling ourselves that they don't matter, and our need to reach out to others gradually disappears until it becomes almost unthinkable to be with them. Learn to love those you feel yourself wanting to shun. Learn to empathize with others; develop your curiosity and ultimately your empathy. Don't miss the opportunity to discover the world through the eyes of another; let us taste the authenticity in a point of view different from our own and accept it. Nothing forces us to join it, just enjoy the pleasure of adopting it for a moment. This experience is likely to overwhelm us, to transform our vision of the world, and to develop both our sensitivity and our tolerance.

By adapting these ways, we learn to show a real interest in the other, to accept and love them. We arouse their own curiosity in turn, and their desire to reach out toward their fellow humans.

⇒Affirmations Station ⇐

Affirmations adapted from the words of Iyanla Vanzant, Lúcia Xavier, Audre Lorde, and Ella Baker.

+ I'm willing to look at my darkness so that it empowers me to change.

+ The threats are real, the challenges are big, but I don't plan on giving up.

+ I am deliberate and afraid of nothing.

✦ I am a friend to other girls: that friend who sees the first tear falling, holds the second tear, and prevents the third.

✦ I give light so that people can find the way.

✦ I use my strength in the service of my vision.

Badass to the Bone

"The greatest lie ever told about love is that it sets you free."

—**Zadie Smith**, English novelist, essayist, and short-story writer of Jamaican descent; her novel *White Teeth* focuses on Britain's relationship with people from formerly colonized countries

"The heaviness of loss in her heart hadn't eased, but there was room there for humor, too."

—**Nalo Hopkinson**, Jamaican-born Canadian speculative fiction writer and editor; she draws on Caribbean history and language to marry folklore and fantasy in her stories

"No hate has ever unlocked the myriad interlacings—the front of love. Hate is nothing."

—**Marita Bonner**, American writer, essayist, and playwright; one of the many unrecognized female voices of the Harlem Renaissance, she often wrote about gender discrimination within the Black community

"I want to die while you love me,
Oh, who would care to live
Till love has nothing more to ask
And nothing more to give!"

—**Georgia Douglas Johnson**, poet and one of the earliest African American female playwrights; she was a significant figure in the anti-lynching movement, and often wrote about lynching in her work

"The things we truly love stay with us always, locked in our hearts as long as life remains."

—**Josephine Baker**, American-born French entertainer, resistance agent, and civil rights activist; she ended up on the FBI watch list after calling out a club owner for racism

"[Love] is easily the most empty cliché, the most useless word, and at the same time the most powerful human emotion—because hatred is involved in it, too."

—**Toni Morrison**, American novelist, essayist, book editor, and college professor; she published her first book at age thirty-nine and went on to win Nobel and Pulitzer prizes

"Love is mutually feeding each other, not one living on another like a ghoul."

—**Bessie Head**, Motswana writer

"I write you a letter that begins
With I love you and ends with I love you and
Somewhere in the middle is one goodbye for
Every hurt."

—**Patricia Smith**, American poet, spoken-word performer, playwright, author, and teacher; she fell in love with poetry while performing, when she realized there was nothing left to hide behind

When you walk in love, everything becomes an object of love, and everything becomes worthy of the effort of loving it. This extends to everything in the world, even beyond people. The birds, the animals, the trees, rivers, the oceans—the whole planet and its environment, and you begin to see clearly that you are a small piece of creation. You may find you feel less alone. Your heart begins to expand and encompasses everything around you. You'll notice when you begin to foster a genuine love for everyone and everything that your days are much happier as well. You'll still go through rough times, but love has a habit of sustaining you through the darkest times and the biggest challenges. It may take you a while to get there, and you'll find some people just don't want to be loved. That's okay. It's a big world and there's plenty to love about it and in it. Start with those around you, and expand your big brave heart as far as you can. It's a muscle, after all. The more you use it, the stronger it grows.

CHAPTER THREE

Beauty—You Are Vibrant with Strength

"Pretty women wonder where my secret lies.
I'm not cute or built to suit a fashion model's size
But when I start to tell them,
They think I'm telling lies.
I say,
It's in the reach of my arms,
The span of my hips,
The stride of my step,
The curl of my lips.
I'm a woman
Phenomenally.
Phenomenal woman,
That's me."

—**Maya Angelou**, from *Phenomenal Woman*

There's a fire inside of you—one that can bring joy to you and those around you. It's called inner beauty, and you've probably heard of it before: "Your inner beauty never needs makeup. Your outer beauty will capture the eyes; your inner beauty will capture the heart." Make yourself beautiful on the inside and you will look beautiful on the outside. Your physical appearance says nothing (or very little) about your values, your state of mind, your character, or who you really are.

When a badass Black girl taps into her inner beauty, she discovers that she's vibrant with strength—and it makes her even more beautiful and noticeable. Inner beauty feeds your generosity, your sense of responsibility, and your passion. It teaches you humility, too. You learn to question your beliefs by engaging in meaningful conversations and learning from others. And when you discover that your character traits are unpleasant, you learn to accept it and try to improve.

There are many people around us who do not meet the standards of beauty established by society. And yet, these people are *beautiful*! They shine with a kind of light that allows us to see beyond their physical appearance, their hairstyle, their look... We appreciate them for *who* they are!

Reconnect with Your Inner Beauty

"I am not my hair, I am not this skin, I am the soul that lives within."

—**India.Arie**, American singer and songwriter; despite being snubbed by the Grammys, her fan base grew and her album sales increased

"Melanin is an incomparable beauty. From the lightest to the darkest skin tone, Black women are exquisite beauty in every shade. Yes, Black females have that special something that just can't be ignored. We are melanin queens, beautifully created! respect the complexion."

—**Stephanie Lahart**, author, poet, and motivational speaker

In a world that tells you the way you look is all that matters, it can be very difficult to focus on your inner beauty. Black girls are more subject to bullying about their looks than most others because of the society we live in, and chances are if you've been bullied or picked on for your looks, you may have internalized some of the harsh things that have been said to you. You should know that none of those things were true. You are as beautiful as anyone else, both inside and outside. Where beauty really counts is in the things you do and in who you are, regardless of how you look to the rest of the world. But there are many things you can do to remain radiant with beauty. So I wanted to give you a few tips to reconnect with your inner beauty.

A badass Black girl changes her focus. Cut yourself some slack. How often are you mean to yourself? "I'm fat," "I suck," "I'm ugly." Would you say those things to your best friend? Then why are you beating yourself up? Since you were a kid, you've heard it: "Your looks don't make you pretty, it's the person inside who makes you pretty!" You've been taught to see inner beauty *in others*. It's time to make a commitment to see the beauty that exists within yourself. It's time to say: *I accept myself and I love myself as I am. I accept my mistakes. I give myself permission to be vulnerable because I understand that it's the key to increasing harmony in body and mind and reconnecting with my inner beauty.* Once you learn to show yourself some compassion, you open your heart to finding what you truly care about, what makes you *you*, and there is nothing more beautiful than to be aligned with your values. Don't wait for other people to acknowledge how badass you are— tell yourself every day. Give yourself the recognition you deserve by changing your focus. Often, we tend to focus on our weaknesses. Focusing on your strengths is the key to being aligned with your inner beauty and being in harmony with yourself.

A badass Black girl laughs often. Show your sense of humor and add a little sparkle to your everyday life, without resorting to sarcasm or cruelty. Humor loosens tensions, makes sad and pathetic events more bearable, and helps improve friendships and other relationships. Laughing can also reduce your risk of a heart attack by up to 40 percent (that's a *huge* number) and helps your body metabolize blood sugar better. Look on the bright side…and you'll live longer! You don't have to be a comedian to spread this fabulous fun. Your sense of humor, as unique as your fingerprints, enriches the world. Think of a sense of humor as a muscle that needs training every now and then. Laugh and *tune in to happiness.* Maybe you felt it once before— during an afternoon stroll on the beach or while listening to good music. Time stopped, and the rest of the world seemed to fade away. You became fully present and felt fully alive. You felt happy—deeply satisfied. Even for a moment, happiness transforms us for the better. You can't define it or measure it, but you recognize it when it's present, and, surprisingly, without your saying a word, others know it too. We can all feel it. Start noticing what makes you happy and remember to have fun!

A badass Black girl stands up straight and dresses the part.
Posture is important. It's not about being stiff as a stake but about having a flexible, relaxed body position that keeps your spine healthy, your feet firmly planted on the ground, and your knees barely bent. Tuck in your stomach, relax your shoulders, and keep your head and neck in line with your shoulders. Allow your spine to assume a natural position with elegant curves. Instantly, you will be taller and more confident. In addition to mastering your posture, you may also want to *dress the part.* You can use your clothes and your outward appearance to make peace with yourself, but make no mistake: being at peace with your external image does not mean being fashionable and following trends. It means you've found your own style—the one that makes you feel like *you.* Clothes have superpowers—they can help you project a better image of yourself by bringing out your personality and what's unique about you. Your clothes don't have to be expensive and trendy. Just be mindful that, just as showing off your style may boost your confidence, some clothes—stained, damaged, misshapen—have the power to undermine your morale, highlighting

all your physical "flaws" or making you invisible…to the world and to yourself. They may convince you that you are not good enough. You deserve so much better!

≫Affirmations Station ≪

Some affirmations you can use to (re)connect with your inner beauty:

+ I stand up straight and tower over my circumstances.

+ I am beautiful, smart, and kind.

+ I am at peace with my body and physical form.

+ I'm on fire from within.

+ I carry the infinite wisdom of the ages.

+ My inner beauty defines me and who I truly am.

A badass Black girl is authentic. Authenticity is about balance: you can do what is important to you, while respecting others and treating them as equals. It involves knowing and respecting yourself enough to make choices that reflect your priorities while at the same time finding ways, kindly and tactfully, to tell the truth. To become skilled at this, of course, takes a lifetime—you don't become authentic overnight. Start by looking at the areas of your life that are relevant to your values, and step away from activities that have nothing to do with who you want to be. Standing up for yourself while showing empathy to others: that's the most authentic form of beauty.

A badass Black girl shows gratitude. Hopefully, you came from an environment that values good manners and you've been taught to say thank you. But gratitude is not just about good manners. Science shows that being grateful increases your own sense of well-being, and doing so spreads positive vibes around the world. Feeling grateful increases optimism, decreases pain and fatigue, and improves performance in school and work. It makes you more vigilant, more enthusiastic, more determined, and more attentive. As a result, gratitude can be a booster shot for your life, bringing you closer to others—it pushes you to help a friend, coworker, neighbor, or family member struggling with a personal issue. It is about emphasizing the good done around you with kind words. Not only does this type of gratitude uplift your spirits, but it lifts the spirits of others as well. Learn to focus on the positive things, to have gratitude for the little things, to appreciate the gifts and the obstacles in life that are essential to your growth. Once you've recognized the gifts that life has bestowed upon you, then you can share them and *be generous.* Volunteer to babysit a younger sibling. Donate part of your allowance to a good cause. Enjoy the satisfaction that comes from helping others. It's interesting to note that helping others activates areas of the brain that are crucial for planning and organizing daily life. It might even extend your life! In one study, volunteers showed a 60 percent lower mortality rate. Whether you volunteer at the local pet shelter or join with friends to help Habitat for Humanity, there are benefits in letting your inner beauty shine.

Badass to the Bone

"The kind of beauty I want most is the hard-to-get kind that comes from within—strength, courage, dignity."

—**Ruby Dee**, American actress, poet, playwright, screenwriter, journalist, and civil rights activist; she and her husband served as master and mistress of ceremonies for the 1963 March on Washington

"Girls of all kinds can be beautiful—from the thin, plus-sized, short, very tall, ebony to porcelain-skinned; the quirky, clumsy, shy, outgoing, and all in between. It's not easy though, because many people still put beauty into a confining, narrow box. Think outside of the box; pledge that you will look in the mirror and find the unique beauty in you."

—**Tyra Banks**, model and businesswoman

"And my mother again would say to me, 'you can't eat beauty, it doesn't feed you.' And these words plagued and bothered me. I didn't really understand them until finally I realized that beauty was not a thing that I could acquire or consume, it was something that I just had to be."

—**Lupita Nyong'o**, Kenyan-Mexican actress and author; she won an Oscar for her role in *12 Years a Slave* after graduating from the Yale School of Drama

"Trust yourself. Think for yourself. Act for yourself. Speak for yourself. Be yourself. Imitation is suicide."

—**Marva Collins**, American educator; for more than thirty years she ran a high-achieving school in her home out of frustration with the Chicago school system

"I always felt like my value was much more in my intellect than it was in my appearance."

—**Kerry Washington**, American actress, producer, and director; she's well-known for her role as Olivia Pope in *Scandal* and is an avid LGBTQ and human rights activist

"As Black women, we're always given these seemingly devastating experiences—experiences that could absolutely break us. But what the caterpillar calls the end of the world, the master calls the butterfly. What we do as Black women is take the worst situations and create from that point."

—**Viola Davis**, American actress; she is the only African American performer to date to have won Tony, Oscar, and Emmy Awards

"Whatever is bringing you down, get rid of it. Because you'll find that when you're free… your true self comes out."

—**Tina Turner**, American-born Swiss singer, songwriter, dancer, and actress; she left a toxic and abusive relationship and went on to have a thriving career full of love

"You are your best thing."

—**Toni Morrison**, American novelist, essayist, book editor, and college professor

See the Beauty in the World

"The leaves believe such letting go is love, such love is faith, such faith is grace, such grace is God. I agree with the leaves."

—**Lucille Clifton**, American poet, writer and educator; her work highlighted the experiences of Black women

There is beauty everywhere. Once you understand this, the world around you changes in a heartbeat. You can look at an ordinary object and find the beauty in it. You can look at grape leaves covered in caterpillars and imagine a butterfly garden. You may meet someone who—by social norms—might not be "beautiful," only to realize that they are the most charming, witty, and intelligent person you have ever known: the most beautiful. Beauty is not an objective, quantifiable characteristic, like height or weight. Beauty isn't just about physical appearance and, as many point out, it is in the eye of the beholder. A badass Black girl trains her eyes to become more sensitive to the beauty around her, instead of constantly focusing her attention on the world's imperfections. She learns to seek the beauty that exists in her surroundings; she learns to feel it too.

But how? How do you silence your inner critic and learn to see perfection in seemingly imperfect things? Here are some suggestions for increasing your ability to connect with the beauty in your life.

A badass Black girl makes space for beauty. I suggest you start by uncluttering your space and cleaning everything that needs cleaning. Discard or recycle anything you no longer value—someone else might like these items. And because everything that goes on in our physical world becomes a reflection of our psychological world and vice versa, you'll find yourself tidying up on the inside as well, letting your inner beauty shine! You will discover new aspects of yourself that will make you happy, and you will reconnect with the beautiful person that you are.

A badass Black girl surrounds herself with beautiful people. Make a list of all the people you hang out with on a regular basis. Next to their names, write down what you find beautiful about their character and share your notes with them. You will see how energizing it is to appreciate and talk about inner beauty. You may find it easier to make the list for others than for yourself. If so, why not tell them: "I am learning to appreciate beauty. So I made a list of everything I find beautiful about my loved ones. I must admit that I have more difficulty doing it for myself than for others. Would you be so kind as to tell me just one quality you like about me so that I can add it to my list?" The person may be surprised at your request, but know that your initiative could help others as much as it helps you to appreciate what is beautiful. And you may be surprised at the things people see in you. Their observations may help you to take a second, more objective look at yourself through other people's points of view and really see what makes you beautiful to them.

A badass Black girl pays attention. A first glance at something doesn't reveal its essence. What we perceive as "average" can very often turn out to be extraordinary if we care to *really* look, to go beyond the first impression. Also, just because you see something every day doesn't mean it's ordinary. Have you ever observed the speed at which a snowflake falls, listened to the sound of raindrops falling on the roof or the waves breaking on the shore, or smelled the salty smell of the ocean? When was the last time you watched the sun reflecting off an autumn leaf or in the windows of a skyscraper, listened to birdsong, watched a starry sky or a sunset ablaze with all the colors of fire? Take the time to look at all the ordinary beauty of the world around you. Pay attention. Don't walk through life distracted by your thoughts. Notice new buildings, beautiful gardens, quirky and cozy little cafes. You are surrounded by wonders, but you may miss them if you are too busy planning the next day or are overwhelmed by memories of the past. Enjoy the pleasure of sharing a meal with people you know well or not at all, of watching a singer or dancer perform, of smiling back at a stranger. Serene or unleashed, the world is magnificent, and its beauty helps us grow. A badass Black girl has an artist's eye. Look at the world as if you were going to draw it. Learn to savor every moment, every second. Let beauty fill your heart with goodness and then share it with people who cross your path.

As we grow up, we lose the ability to maintain enthusiasm and a sense of discovery. A five-year-old can hear the same story ten times with the same interest, the same excitement as when they first heard it. A young adult can hardly wait more than five seconds before informing everyone that they have heard it all before. Let go of the idea that familiar things are boring and try to see them from a new perspective. Give it a try and you will see that you'll make some remarkable discoveries! Discover the world with eyes wide open and be amazed by what you see around you. Realize that, no matter where you are, whether it is thousands of miles from your house or even in your own neighborhood, everything around us is a source of beauty and deserves our attention, if only for a few minutes a day.

Here are two exercises to make the familiar strange and the strange familiar.

1. Examine a pen like a Martian seeing one for the first time, and try to understand what it is, what it is used for. This leads to looking differently at things you are already familiar with and opens your perceptions.

2. To make the strange familiar, observe a work of art that seems bizarre to you and try to find familiar elements: the shape of the eyes that reminds us of someone, a landscape in the background that evokes a familiar place. This will allow you to go beyond the first feeling, to see the positive in the negative.

A badass Black girl sees the beauty in herself. Seeing the beauty in others starts with seeing the beauty in yourself. Have you ever thought about how amazing you are? Your body is an amazing biological organism that can breathe, move, distinguish over a million shades of colors, digest food, and often heal on its own. You have the capacity to love, to create, to laugh, to imagine, to feel compassion toward other human beings, and to give life. Your thoughts, beliefs, emotions, and actions create your reality and shape your life. You are the greatest miracle ever created. You are unique. You should never forget it. We spend our time wanting to be amazed and envying others, but we must realize how magical our own life is. Every moment can be dotted with sparks that make it memorable.

Every day, make a habit of surrounding yourself with beauty and looking for it inside and outside yourself. This will quickly transform your life. You will find it easier to know what you want, what is important to you, what really makes your heart happy, and you will develop more self-confidence.

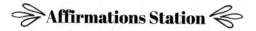

Affirmations Station

Some affirmations you can use to see the beauty in the world:

+ I live in beauty and in light in all ways.

+ I see the beauty of the world around me.

+ The world is beautiful, and I am beautiful.

+ I wake up every morning ready for a new day of exciting possibilities.

+ Beauty flows with me as the beauty of the world flows in me.

+ My world is beautiful.

A badass Black girl discovers the creative beauty that exists in her. One way to let your inner beauty shine is to develop your creativity. Creative people are determined, flexible, and imaginative. They are problem solvers. Open and curious, they express themselves better than everyone else, and are more apt to come up with new ideas. Unexpected situations, doubt, and uncertainty do not scare them, because their creativity allows them to bounce back and adapt to all situations.

You can develop your creativity by incorporating new habits into your daily life.

+ **Get into DIY.** Coloring, knitting, sewing… In addition to being good for morale, DIY helps stimulate one's imagination and inventiveness. A badass Black girl dedicates time to hands-on activities in order to develop her creativity. DIY activities help you unleash creative self-confidence. This helps you to stop being afraid of failure and dare to believe in your projects!

+ **Get out of your comfort zone and maintain your curiosity.** Routine stifles creativity. Get out of your comfort zone and face the unknown. Feeding your imagination regularly is essential for unleashing your creativity to its fullest potential. Forget about Netflix. Attend shows, concerts, exhibits, conferences…even if virtually. Discover new things.

+ **Take a walk.** According to researchers at Stanford University, walking for a few minutes promotes the emergence of new ideas.

+ **Live in the moment.** Take a few minutes every day to really listen and feel your surroundings. This contemplative break will encourage the emergence of creative ideas. It is also a good idea to meditate. A study by researchers at Leiden University found that people who regularly meditate were more apt to come up with new and original ideas. So don't hesitate to incorporate fifteen minutes of meditation into your morning routine!

+ **Write.** Practiced regularly, writing exercises are real boosters of creativity. Just take a piece of paper and a pencil, and write everything that comes to mind, without judgment. As the days go by, your ideas will become better organized and flow from you faster. Writing regularly also helps you acquire persistence.

+ **Get bored.** Did you know that boredom is conducive to creativity? Indeed, when you do nothing, your brain takes the opportunity to sort out your thoughts and make connections that will bring out new ideas. Therefore, don't hesitate to leave a few holes in your schedule!

+ **Take care of yourself.** When you are comfortable with your body and mind, you create a climate conducive to the emergence of new ideas. To develop your creativity, take care of yourself with a balanced diet, regular sports, and activities that make you happy. Unleash your creativity!

Badass to the Bone

"To know how much there is to know is the beginning of learning to live."

—**Dorothy West**, American novelist and short-story writer; best known for her collection of stories and essays *The Richer, the Poorer*, which highlights the complexities of middle-class African Americans

"Never be limited by other people's limited imaginations… If you adopt their attitudes, then the possibility won't exist because you'll have already shut it out… You can hear other people's wisdom, but you've got to reevaluate the world for yourself."

—**Mae Jemison**, American engineer, physician, and former NASA astronaut; she was the first African American woman in the NASA astronaut program and the first African American woman in space

"Just don't give up what you're trying to do. Where there is love and inspiration, I don't think you can go wrong."

—**Ella Fitzgerald**, American jazz singer

"Miracles happen all the time.
We're here, aren't we?"

—**Marilyn Nelson**, award-winning American poet and children's book author; the first poem she ever wrote was to honor her little brother who had passed away

"No Black woman writer in this culture can write 'too much.' Indeed, no woman writer can write 'too much'.…No woman has ever written enough."

—**bell hooks**, American author, professor, feminist, and social activist

"When you put love out in the world, it travels, and it can touch people and reach people in ways that we never even expected."

—**Laverne Cox**, American actress and LGBTQ+ advocate

"Paradise is One's own place, One's own people, One's own world, Knowing and known, Perhaps even Loving and loved."

—**Octavia E. Butler**, American science fiction author; she went on to write many stories despite being told by an aunt that Black people can't be writers

So, Beautiful (yes, you!), it's easy to let your inner strength shine for you. If you make a practice of focusing on true beauty, you'll find yourself radiating it and embodying it. The world needs more people who are willing to be themselves regardless of what others think of them. So don't pay any attention to the negative, cruel things some people might say. Instead, pay attention to the good in everyone and, most importantly, in yourself. In no time at all, you'll *feel* as beautiful as you are. Others will notice it too. You can't really hide what you are, can you? There's no fun in that and no authenticity. You can't fake beauty; you just have to trust that you—as you are right now—are equally as beautiful as everyone around you. Don't forget to let others know how beautiful they are too, in all their unique, inspiring, ways. People are like reflections of each other, and if you can see and share what you see with others, you'll see it and feel it in yourself too. Now, be brave, and you glow, girl!

CHAPTER FOUR

Work—You're the Architect of Your Badass Life

"I've learned that 'making a living' is not the same as 'making a life.'"

—**Maya Angelou**, American poet, memoirist, and civil rights activist

We all have to work. Whether you're completing homework, helping with chores at home, just got your first job, or are working on a personal project—it's work, work, work. I'm pretty sure you sometimes wonder (maybe grudgingly), "Why am I doing this?" Most of us acknowledge the necessity of work (because, um, grades or money), but you might want to spend some quality time thinking about what truly makes you happy, so that you (eventually!) dedicate most of your hours doing what is truly meaningful, what keeps you engaged and motivated, and what allows for the kind of relationships you're interested in. Every Black girl out there will agree: there's nothing like the sweet, sweet sense of personal accomplishment.

Dream Big

"Never underestimate the power of dreams and the influence of the human spirit. We are all the same in this notion. The potential for greatness lives within each of us."

—**Wilma Rudolph**, American sprinter; she overcame physical disabilities to become a world-record-holding Olympic champion in track and field

We're happier when our work goes hand in hand with our dreams or what we consider to be our calling in life. My father was a college professor, and one of my tasks at home was to help him type his lectures, and sometimes he'd ask me to assess his lesson plans. I was thirteen, but he trusted me to provide valuable feedback, and, because I knew deep down that I myself would be a teacher one day, I enjoyed every minute of our time "working" together. Years later, I became a teacher and a college professor and those early experiences with my father helped me understand my job, because I learned early the importance of study and preparation, not just as a student but as a classroom leader. Prior to helping him, I hadn't realized how much work teachers put into preparation. From an early age, we Black girls nurture big dreams. But these dreams will only become real if we actively plan concrete steps to carry them out. That's why goals are important. Goals help us realize our dreams. A badass Black girl sets personal goals to give meaning to everything she does, and to keep motivated and efficient on a daily basis. Affirmations can help, because they keep us mindful of our goals and help us focus on the outcome we desire. It can be easy to lose track of your goals in the rush of day-to-day life. Affirmations help us slow down and pay attention to what we really want.

Maybe you've already set a few goals (some of us are naturally good at goal setting!), but it's okay if you haven't done so yet. It's never too late. Just remember that setting goals allows you to give meaning to your life. When you have goals, you know exactly why you get up in the morning. You know where you're going, and you come closer to achieving success every day. If you're forced to sell raffle tickets at an event you don't care about, for example, it's a different experience than if you're working on a goal: sell x number of raffle tickets to fund a field trip for your awesome youth group. Goals bring enthusiasm; they motivate us by giving more meaning to what we do.

Ava DuVernay is a writer, producer, director, and distributor of independent films. She's always been focused on one thing: telling the stories of Black folks. Her focus led her to success. Renae L. Bluitt is another filmmaker who champions Black women's representation in the media. By concentrating on one area, both women are able to practice a specialty in filmmaking. Remember, specialization leads to mastery. You may not be ready to specialize just yet, but once you figure out what you'd like to do with your life, it will help to find an area of expertise that calls to you.

Affirmations are a good way to remind yourself that you are trying to find direction in life and that you trust the process of finding your way through what can be a confusing world.

+ **Know what is important.** When you have goals, you know what you want. You take stock of what's important to you and what isn't. Or rather, you prioritize the different components of your life. "Should I spend more time practicing for my piano recital, learning about coding, or helping with the soup kitchen?" Setting goals for yourself will help you see things more clearly. You can then refocus on what really matters to you. Mariya Russell, the first Black woman to earn a Michelin star, knew from a young age that she would become a chef. She made it a point to perfect cooking soul food and Midwestern staples like mashed potatoes, fried chicken, and casseroles. When you make an affirmation linked to a goal, it can help crystalize your path for you so that your direction is much clearer and sharper.

✦ **Better manage your time.** Growing up, I had friends outside of my age group. In addition to hanging out with teenagers like myself, I spent time with my older sisters and their friends and with some of my neighbors, and it became clear to me very early that time waits for nobody. Time is something we never get back—it's a cliché because it's true. Setting goals helps us optimize our time; with a goal in mind, we carefully plan our days.

✦ **Boost your self-esteem.** Achieving goals that we set for ourselves brings us personal satisfaction and increased self-esteem. Self-esteem is an essential element in personal development and fulfillment. Of course, having confidence in yourself and being proud of what you do does not mean that you have to be arrogant and disrespectful toward others. Self-esteem is a strength. *Black-ish* star Marsai Martin is the youngest executive producer in history. In an interview with the *LA Times*, she talks about confidence. "Believe in yourself," she says. "Push to your highest limit. Be confident that you can do it. If you take that one push to do it, then God's got the rest. Just leave it up to him."

Affirmations Station

Affirmations adapted from the words of Madame C. J. Walker, Lisa Nichols, Shonda Rhimes, Maya Angelou, and Oprah Winfrey.

✦ I make my own living and my own opportunity. I don't sit down and wait for the opportunities to come. I get up and make them.

✦ I am the designer of my destiny; I am the author of my story.

✦ I am smart, I am talented, I take advantage of the opportunities that come my way, and I work really, really hard.

✦ I am the dream; I accept and acknowledge my own brilliance.

✦ I think like a queen. A queen is not afraid to fail. Failure is another stepping-stone to greatness.

Badass to the Bone

"Instead of looking at the past, I put myself ahead twenty years and try to look at what I need to do now in order to get there then."

—**Diana Ross**, American singer, actress, and record producer with a career spanning over six decades

"I always believed that when you follow your heart or your gut, when you really follow the things that feel great to you, you can never lose, because settling is the worst feeling in the world."

—**Rihanna**, Barbadian singer, songwriter, actress, businesswoman, and philanthropist

"You wanna know what scares people? Success. When you don't make moves and when you don't climb up the ladder, everybody loves you because you're not competition."

—**Nicki Minaj**, Trinidadian-American singer, songwriter, actress, and model; she once dropped out of a concert in Saudi Arabia, protesting the arrest of a prominent women's right activist there

"There have been so many people who have said to me, 'You can't do that,' but I've had an innate belief that they were wrong. Be unwavering and relentless in your approach."

—**Halle Berry**, American actress; she was the first African American woman to win an Academy Award in 2002

"Be passionate and move forward with gusto every single hour of every single day until you reach your goal."

—**Ava DuVernay**, American writer, producer, director, and distributor of independent films

"Surround yourself with only people who are going to lift you higher."

—**Oprah Winfrey**, American talk show host, actress, television producer, media executive, and philanthropist

"I'm convinced that we Black women possess a special indestructible strength that allows us to not only get down, but to get up, to get through, and to get over."

—**Janet Jackson**, American singer, songwriter, actress, and dancer

"Dreams are lovely. But they are just dreams. Fleeting, ephemeral, pretty. But dreams do not come true just because you dream them. It's hard work that makes things happen. It's hard work that creates change."

—**Shonda Rhimes**, American television producer, television and film writer, and author

"When opportunity presents itself, grab it. Hold on tight and don't let go."

—**Celia Cruz**, Afro-Cuban salsa singer; through her outspoken voice, presence, and beautiful dark skin, she gave space for Afro-Latinos to proudly embrace their diverse and beautiful lineage

See It for Yourself

"I always believed that if you set out to be successful, then you already were."

—**Katherine Dunham**, African American dancer, choreographer, author, educator, anthropologist, and social activist; she went on a forty-seven-day hunger strike in support of Haitian refugees

It is important to think, *really* think, about things. I don't mean the five-second thought that brushes your mind, or the five-minute conversation with your girl Anaya. Do some *real* introspection and write down your thoughts! Then use the daily affirmations that are in line with what you're trying to accomplish. South Sudanese-Australian supermodel Adut Akech Bior spent a lot of time thinking about ways to make a difference in the world. A former child refugee herself, she now works with the UN to help refugees.

When it comes to strategically thinking about your goal and your personal mission in life, I suggest a technique called mind mapping, which allows you to remind yourself of your goals and to hold yourself accountable for the actions to be taken to achieve them.

Mind mapping is a visual representation of your ideas; it is both creative (make it as pretty as you want) and organized (the sections are listed below). Although you can create a mind map for almost anything, in this case it's all about *you.*

A mind map includes your values, your strengths, your goals, your required learning, what you want to have, and what you want to be.

Your values. You might be telling yourself that this part is the easiest. But do you really know what your values are? What you are not prepared to compromise on? List five of your most important values.

Project YM has used the following "What would you do?" scenarios to encourage teenagers to think about their values.

1. You invite four of your close friends over to watch a movie with you. One of your friends invited another friend, so there are six of you including yourself. You only have five cans of soda and want to give everyone drinks, but you're one can shy. How do you handle it?

2. One of your classmates is mean to you every day. He jostles you in the hallway and calls you hurtful names. He knocks your books out of your hands and everyone laughs at you when you have to pick them up. You've reached a breaking point. How do you handle it?

3. If you caught your BFF's boyfriend kissing another girl, what would you do?

4. You find a wallet with two thousand dollars in it. Do you try to find the owner?

5. You see some younger kids picking on another kid, do you step in? What if the kids were older?

6. A cashier at the store near your house mistakenly gives you ten dollars too much change. What do you do?

7. Someone in an online group you belong to posts something offensive. Do you say something to the person? Do you contact a group moderator? Send the person a direct message? Or do you do nothing because it's a group post?

Other elements of the mind map are:

Your strengths. What are you good at? Your strengths don't need to be very specific or tangible. I, for example, consider myself to be creative, and I consider this strength to be part of my top five. Remember that success *does not* mean strength. You might get lucky and ace a social science test—that doesn't mean you're good at social science. Conversely, you could be very good at painting, but you've never encountered success because you've never shown your work to anyone. Also, remember that the concept of success is subjective to each person. While some writers consider themselves successful only after selling thousands of copies of their book, others equate the completion of the book itself with success. Affirmations can help you turn your strengths into successes by encouraging you to focus on achievements related to areas where you feel you are strongest. They can also encourage you to build strength in areas where you might feel you are weaker by focusing your intent on improvement.

Your goals. In theory, there is no limit to the number of goals you might want to achieve. However, one of the main reasons people don't reach their goals is because they have too many of them, don't know where to start, and end up thinking they're unrealistic. Stick to only a few goals—and make sure they are SMART goals.

Specific	What *exactly* do I want to happen?
Measurable	I will know I have reached my goal when…
Attainable	With hard work, is it possible to reach this goal by the deadline?
Realistic and Relevant	My goal is important enough for me to put a plan into action. I will follow this specific plan to reach my goal…
Time Bound	I will reach my goal by…

1. *Your goal must be specific and clear.* You should be able to write it in one or two sentences. A stranger should be able to read what you have written and understand what it is. This implies understanding exactly what success (or failure) will look like. Therefore, make a commitment to yourself. Be accountable and specific.

2. *Your goal must be measurable.* You must be able to track your progress. And in order to track your progress, you need to be able to quantify it. Yeah… math… all these numbers! But hear me out: Saying "I guess I did okay" *is not* good enough if you haven't reached your goal. You have to know how to recognize success. Your goal should be measurable and quantifiable. Mary McLeod Bethune is a good example of a trailblazer who kept her own goals in mind. In 1936, she was appointed to a government post when President Franklin Delano Roosevelt named her Director of Negro Affairs at the National Youth Administration. Having met that goal, Bethune didn't stop there. She also opened a boarding school for Black girls that eventually merged with another school to become Bethune-Cookman College.

3. *Your goal must be achievable.* Start small. A small success will boost your motivation and encourage you to keep up the momentum. Your goal must be achievable. Ambitious, yes— but achievable. For example, if you are not a runner, but would like to be more physically active, you might choose to set a goal to run a half mile in two weeks' time.

4. *Your goal must be realistic.* An achievable goal might be unrealistic based on your environment and your capacities. Is running a marathon achievable? Sure, people run marathons all the time. Is it realistic for you to run a marathon next week if you haven't exercised a day in your life? Nope. A seventy-year-old man and a twenty-year-old who both want to run the South Beach Marathon are not in the same situation despite having the same goal.

5. *Your goal must be time bound.* You may have a daily, weekly, monthly, or yearly goal. But whatever the case, you need to set an *end date*. So, for example, if you set a goal to run a half mile in two weeks' time and enjoyed meeting that goal, you may decide to go into training for that marathon by the end of

the year. This will give you plenty of time to build the stamina needed to complete the marathon.

Affirmations Station

✦ I recklessly believe in myself.

✦ I believe in my heart what I know to be true about myself.

✦ I don't believe in failure. It is not a failure if I enjoy the process.

✦ I have all the qualities in me to achieve my goals.

✦ I will achieve great things.

✦ I trust my choices and move forward in this direction.

Badass to the Bone

"Everything that happens to you is a reflection of what you believe about yourself. We cannot outperform our level of self-esteem. We cannot draw to ourselves more than we think we are worth."

—**Iyanla Vanzant**, American inspirational speaker, lawyer, New Thought spiritual teacher, author, life coach, and television personality

"Never be afraid to sit awhile and think."

—**Lorraine Hansberry**, American playwright and writer

"There's so much creativity in brokenness. Brokenness will have you making it work."

—**Issa Rae**, American actress, writer, and producer

"The only way you can grow is to let yourself make mistakes and create contradictions."

—**Nikki Giovanni**, American poet, writer, commentator, activist, and educator; she's well known for having written over two dozen books and is one of Oprah Winfrey's Twenty-Five Living Legends

"I really think a champion is defined not by their wins but by how they can recover when they fall."

—**Serena Williams**, American professional tennis player; she has won over twenty-two Grand Slam singles titles, more than any man or woman during the Open Era

"Success is only meaningful and enjoyable if it feels like your own."

—**Michelle Obama**, American attorney, author, and former First Lady of the United States; she fights and speaks adamantly for education as a fundamental necessity for living fully

"Without faith, nothing is possible. With it, nothing is impossible."

—**Mary McLeod Bethune**, American educator, stateswoman, philanthropist, humanitarian, womanist, and civil rights activist; well known for starting a private university, she also founded the National Council for Negro Women

Because goals need to be time bound, it's important to understand the difference between a long-term goal, a medium-term goal, and a short-term goal. It's quite easy: let's say for instance that you want to attend an Ivy League school in four years; that's a *long-term goal*. What are you going to do this year to get close to that goal? Maybe you'll run for student government. That's a *medium-term goal*. What are you going to do *today*? Maybe you'll study for the geometry exam to keep your grades up. That's a *short-term goal.*

Once you've established your long-term goal, focus on the short term by determining concrete actions that you can take. Little by little, as you learn more about your strengths and values, you may have to redefine your medium-term and long-term goals. A badass Black girl closely monitors her progress.

+   She writes down and actively imagines having achieved these goals.

+   She reviews her goals and reassess priorities from time to time.

The affirmations you say will help you by keeping you positive and concentrated on meeting all your goals. They're a little like a spell you say to yourself, but with positive results and without the magic. (Or maybe there's some magic that gets pulled from you when you repeat them.) The words themselves have no power. It's the repetition and your follow-up with actions after you start saying the affirmations that give them their strength.

The last steps of your mind map include:

Your required learning. To achieve the goals you just listed, are there things you need to learn? For example, if your goal is to get your driver's license this year, what courses or training should you take? List your answers in priority order. The first item on your list should be the first item you check off as completed.

A lot of experts are willing to share their experience with others. Lena Waithe was the first Black woman to win a Primetime Emmy for Outstanding Writing in a Comedy Series. She believes in paying it forward: "I have a ton of mentees," she told *Vanity Fair.* "They're all people of color. Some of them are poor. And I'm just trying to help them learn how to be great writers. And for those that have become really good writers, I help them get representation. And those that have representation, I want to help get them jobs. That to me is a form of activism."

Who are the mentors you could learn from?

What you want to have. What will your goals get you? Maybe you want to become an expert at designing shoes like Aurora James. Whatever it is, manifest it on your map.

What you want to be. Again, what do you want out of your goals ultimately? You might want to become a leader and inspire others. You might want to be an innovator like Ari Melenciano who brings together art, science, history, and Black culture. She is changing the world, helping to build a STEAM curriculum that is culturally relevant in New York. "I think much of my work intentionally serves as a mirror for the beauty, capability, and innovation of Black culture," Melenciano told *Insider*. "To remind my community, in case they ever forget or are told otherwise, how abundant we are."

Take Action

"How dull it is to have people defining you."

—**Octavia E. Butler**, American science fiction author

Use your map. Your map is useless if you do not use it. When you are faced with a big decision, ask yourself:

+ Is my decision in line with my core values?

+ Will I be using my strengths?

+ Will this decision help me achieve my goals?

+ Will I learn something useful?

✦   Will it contribute to what I want to have and what I want to be in my life?

All these questions should be answered in connection with your map before making your choice. You make better decisions when they are aligned with your goals now and in the future. You'll also be more motivated, more efficient, and less stressed. A visual representation of our goals makes it easier for us to think about the key factors essential to our success.

Affirmations Station

✦   I feel confident about my success; I believe in myself and in my abilities.

✦   Every day, I assert myself more and more, with kindness and authenticity.

✦   Every day, I give myself the right to shine more and more.

✦   I have the strength to make my dreams come true, and every step I take increases my strength.

✦   I have within me all the resources necessary to succeed in all my projects.

✦   I deserve to receive all the gifts in the universe.

Badass to the Bone

"Don't another person come up to me and say 'you go girl.' No, you go!"

—**Maxine Waters**, American congresswoman

"Women in particular need to keep an eye on their physical and mental health, because if we're scurrying to and from appointments and errands, we don't have a lot of time to take care of ourselves. We need to do a better job of putting ourselves higher on our own 'to do' list."

—**Michelle Obama**, American attorney, author, and former First Lady of the United States

"It is better to look ahead and prepare than to look back and regret."

—**Jackie Joyner-Kersee**, Olympic legend and gold medalist; she was one of the first women to score more than seven thousand points in the heptathlon event

"You can and should set your own limits and clearly articulate them. This takes courage, but it is also liberating and empowering, and often earns you new respect."

—**Rosalind Brewer**, American businesswoman, COO of Starbucks

"No one can figure out your worth but you."

—**Pearl Bailey**, American actress, humorist, and singer

"I feel myself becoming the fearless person I have dreamt of being. Have I arrived? No. But I'm constantly evolving and challenging myself to be unafraid to make mistakes."

—**Janelle Monáe**, American singer, songwriter, rapper, actress, and producer

"When I was younger, there was something in me. I had passion. I may not have known what I was going to do with that passion, but there was something—and I still feel it. It's this little engine that roars inside of me and I just want to keep going and going."

—**Sheila Johnson**, American businesswoman, cofounder of BET; she was the first African American woman to own/partner in more than three professional sports franchises

"We have to nurture our young women and understand the beauty and the strength of being a woman. It's kind of a Catch-22: Strength in women isn't appreciated, and vulnerability in women isn't appreciated. It's like, 'What the hell do you do?' What you do is you don't allow anyone to dictate who you are."

—**Jada Pinkett Smith**, American actress, screenwriter, producer, talk show host, businesswoman, and singer-songwriter; she has partnered with organizations to build wells in several African countries

Do or Do Not. There Is No Try.

Those are the words of Master Yoda in *The Empire Strikes Back*. Now that you have a map and know what activities you should focus on, here are some tips to be more efficient when working on a project.

Decide what you want. Use your mind map to express your goals to yourself clearly and in detail. Do not let your negative thoughts or inner critic stop you from working toward what you really want. As soon as you set a goal, your subconscious will wake up and help you reach it. You will then attract the right people, and life will put you in the right situations. Black girl magic! Think about the larger picture—and then work on a series of small steps to get where you want. By planning for the long term, but focusing on one small step at a time, you'll see that everything becomes much more meaningful. Mari Copeny (a.k.a. Little Miss Flint) was concerned about the quality of water in her hometown of Flint, Michigan, so she wrote to President Obama to make him aware of the problem with the city's drinking supply. He responded, and in the two years following their correspondence, Mari had donated to school kids over a thousand backpacks filled with supplies. She also became the youngest ever youth ambassador for the Women's March. Remember to dedicate yourself to one task at a time. Multitasking is taxing on the brain. You are neither a robot nor a computer. Take the time to complete your projects step by step.

Believe in yourself. Be deeply convinced that you have all it takes to achieve your goals—to launch any project close to your heart. Marley Dias was tired of reading children's books with white boys as protagonists, so she launched the #1000BlackGirlBooks campaign, with the aim of finding a thousand books with young Black heroines. Since then, she has worked to donate books and organized with educators to promote diversity in reading. Yeah, you'll be stressed out, you'll face trials and tribulations, but don't let this get you down. Remember that your determination will allow you to make some of your dreams come true. If you are more motivated to do your tasks, there's a much better chance they'll be done well.

Stimulate your brain. According to scientists, whatever goal you set, your subconscious mind will work day and night to make it happen, *if* your goal is measurable. If no concrete criteria exists, it will be difficult for your brain to get to work; it will perceive your dream as a wish, a good idea, but not as something that requires concrete action. Start small—focus on goals that are achievable, and train your brain to respond positively.

Dr. Shirley Jackson always kept her goals in mind. Dr. Jackson became the first Black woman to earn a PhD from MIT in theoretical physics, and only the second Black woman in US History to receive a doctorate in physics. President Barack Obama awarded her the National Medal of Science in 2015. Since then, she was hired on as president at Rensselaer Polytechnic Institute and became the first Black woman at the helm of a top-tier research university. While at Rensselaer, she's raised over one billion dollars for philanthropic causes!

Research shows that it takes an average of twenty-one days for our brain to acquire a new habit. Focus on your measurable goal for twenty-one days and you'll be well on your way to reaching it. Repeat your affirmations twenty-one days in a row and train your brain to respond positively.

Use your peak hours. Friday is often the day of the week when it becomes difficult to be effective. We tend to slack in the afternoon because we're over the week already. Know how to schedule your work for the hours when you are most productive. Personally, I like to focus on the tedious tasks first thing in the morning, and early in the week too, when my motivation is at its peak.

Get organized. Keep your environment tidy—clutter affects productivity. Get your schedule organized as well: use a planner or a to-do list and plan your day the night before. Suddenly, all the ideas in your head will start making sense; you'll clearly see the end goal. Now it's about prioritizing: put the most important tasks at the top of the list, along with those that can be completed quickly. And try not to shy away from this list until every item has been checked off. Being organized will allow you to minimize the time spent on meaningless tasks in favor of meaningful ones.

Affirmations Station

+ I don't have to be perfect; I just need to be myself.

+ Just as I am, with no alterations, I am enough.

+ As I love myself, I allow others to love me too.

+ I accept all the blessings of the universe.

+ I control my choices and my life.

+ I'm ready to try new things.

Badass to the Bone

"I don't harp on the negative because if you do, then there's no progression. There's no forward movement. You got to always look on the bright side of things, and we are in control. Like, you have control over the choices you make."

—**Taraji P. Henson**, American actress, director, and author; at thirty-one she had a breakout role on *Baby Boy*, and throughout her career she has advocated for mental health awareness

"Don't ever make decisions based on fear. Make decisions based on hope and possibility. Make decisions based on what should happen, not what shouldn't."

—**Michelle Obama**, American attorney, author, and former First Lady of the United States

"I have chosen to no longer be apologetic for my femaleness and my femininity. And I want to be respected in all of my femaleness because I deserve to be."

—**Chimamanda Ngozi Adichie**, Nigerian writer

"I never intended to become a run-of-the-mill person."

—**Barbara Jordan**, American lawyer, educator, and politician; the first Black woman in the Texas Senate, she later extended the Voting Rights Act for Hispanic, Native, and Asian Americans

"If your neighbor looks at you like they don't enjoy the key you're singing in, look right back, bless them, and keep on singing."

—**Odetta Holmes**, American singer, songwriter, actress, musician, and civil and human rights activist; often referred to as "The Voice of the Civil Rights Movement"

"I am not a quitter. I will fight until I drop. It is just a matter of having some faith in the fact that as long as you are able to draw breath in the universe, you have a chance."

—**Cicely Tyson**, award-winning American actress and former fashion model; she actively chooses not to take roles that depict Black women in a negative light

"In every aspect of our lives, we are always asking ourselves, how am I of value? What is my worth? Yet I believe that worthiness is our birthright."

—**Oprah Winfrey**, American talk show host, actress, television producer, media executive, and philanthropist

More tips:

Take breaks. Breaks are essential for the efficiency of your work. They allow you to relax, even for a moment. When you find that you can no longer focus on your work—take a break! If you don't, fatigue may take over and you will work more slowly and therefore with less efficiency. It is advisable to take two breaks a day, one in the morning, one in the afternoon. We have a limited ability to concentrate: regardless of our involvement in work, our brain tires! Breaks are not a waste of time. On the contrary, they allow you to take a step back and restart by being more productive. Get something to drink, take a walk… Stop working whenever the need arises. Don't push too hard. Knowing how to stop doesn't mean taking breaks every ten minutes, though: you also have to be reasonable.

"In order for you to be able to execute all of those different qualities as a woman and as a person, you have to take care of yourself."

—**Tia Mowry-Hardrict**, American actress and author; she has used her
   YouTube channel to bring awareness to racial issues

Avoid distractions. So many things call for our attention—pop up
notifications, direct messages, phone calls… Turn it off!

Widely regarded as a ballet prodigy, Misty Copeland was dancing *en
pointe* within her first three months of taking a dance class at thirteen.
She was performing professionally in just over a year, making her an
extreme rarity in the sport. She didn't allow anything to distract her
from her goal: becoming the first Black woman to be the American
Ballet Theatre's principal dancer.

Be like Misty.

Adopt a healthy lifestyle. Your health is linked to your
productivity. A healthy and balanced diet, regular exercise, and a
good-night sleep remain the keys to success. Exercise is particularly
important if you spend a lot of time in front of the screen; it helps with
stress and helps you focus better. Sleep deprivation affects the quality
of your work; doctors recommend seven or eight hours of sleep each
night in order to reorganize your thoughts. Many health experts
recommend meditation as well.

Play well with others. Look for people who share your interests
and your goals. Take turns working on some of the repetitive and
less important tasks so that you have time to focus on innovative
solutions. Learn from them as much as they learn from you. What
could be more rewarding than sharing knowledge? It is a rewarding
experience, explaining something that may seem obvious to you
to someone who does not know it—and learning from them at the
same time.

London Breed, San Francisco's first Black female mayor, saw homelessness in San Francisco as a major problem. In response, she declared a shelter crisis and, working with others, came up with plans to add a thousand shelter beds in 2020. She also focuses on mental health, fighting drug addiction and paying high school interns from her city for their work.

If you enjoy what you are doing, and can work on things that interest you, work doesn't have to feel like a drudge. The good thing about work is that if your first few jobs don't turn out the way you want them to, you can always try something new and reinvent yourself. The affirmations in this chapter should help you keep focused on your goals and intentions. Be sure to practice saying them every day, and in no time you'll be on your way to changing the world, one little step at a time.

CHAPTER FIVE

Family—
The One We're Given,
the One We Choose

"Alone, all alone
Nobody, but nobody
Can make it out here alone."

—**Maya Angelou**, American poet, memoirist, and civil rights activist

Family has a great impact on who we are—and on who we become. Our family shapes the way we think and behave, our outlook on life, and the decisions we make. It defines us. Within our family, we learn the basic rules of living together, along with the skills we need to develop our individual potential and deal with the future demands of being an adult.

During the years before Lincoln signed the Emancipation Proclamation ending slavery, "family" was a tenuous idea in most Black households. Fathers and mothers were sold off to different plantation owners, often miles away. Children were also often separated from their parents, either by being sold, or by being put to work on another area of the plantation. In order to keep the bonds of some kind of family, Black people bestowed honorific titles like "auntie," "uncle," and others on people who may not have been blood relatives but who were close friends and served as a surrogate family. The roots of this custom come to us from Africa, where it was considered an honor to be held in such high esteem by someone outside of the family. The custom of holding the utmost respect for the oldest members of the family was also adopted at around the same time. Probably because the eldest family members had been through the most painful situations and had gained the most wisdom.

Even today, many members of the Black community continue the practice of bestowing honorific family titles on friends they are close to and who they look up to with respect. Despite what the media would have you believe, ties in the Black community are tight, and bonds run deep. "Brother" and "sister" are words with multiple meanings to us.

Show Them You Care

"There is nothing to make you like other human beings so much as doing things for them."
—**Zora Neale Hurston**, American author, anthropologist, and filmmaker

Don't take it for granted that your family members know how you feel about them. Even if they do know, it never hurts to show love to your family. Beyond the magic words ("I love you"), there are small gestures you can make to express how you feel. Love is not about how you act in public—when others are watching. Affection at home, in the form of a hug or kind words, is important. Hugs and kisses are not overrated. We all need the physical contact of those around us to feel loved, cared for, and respected. When you physically connect with a loved one, you are also making an emotional connection. Don't hesitate to touch the arm, shoulder, hand, or head of a family member while talking to them. Hold their hand while you're walking in the park or give them a hug when you see each other after being apart all day.

Maybe you're not the demonstrative type and you think that saying "I love you" out loud is a little corny. In this case, leave a letter on your sister's nightstand or a card on the refrigerator door, send a text to Dad on his cell phone, or an email letting Grandma know you are thinking of her. Small gifts that don't necessarily cost a lot of money are also a great way to show you care. In fact, it's much better if you make them yourself or if they represent something important to you. Spending quality time with our family is another way to show them we love them. Put down the phone. Watch a movie together. Play cards or board games. Dance and laugh aloud.

Another great way to say how you feel about your family is to praise them for a job well done. When was the last time you showed interest in your brother's basketball game or chess tournament? When was the last time you showed gratitude for Aunt Gilda's delicious dinner? If Mom came home excited about her day at work, did you ask her about it? In addition to praising people at home, you might also want to help make their job easier—help keep the house clean and tidy. Do things without being specifically asked, and surprise your parents! Learn to respect and care for your elders, to practice good manners, and to avoid backtalk.

Asking for forgiveness when you're wrong is another way to show love in the family. Remind them that, despite your mistake, you care about them. In addition, do your best to fix the situation. The reverse is also true. Everyone makes mistakes sometimes, and it's important to forgive your family members if they slip up or have a rough day and say something harsh. Letting them know you understand and forgive them is another way of saying you love them. We'll discuss more serious behavior later in the chapter, but for the everyday kind of mistakes people make, forgiveness will make you both feel better.

Affirmations Station

+ I love and accept myself completely.

+ My heart is filled with love.

+ I sow love and I reap love.

+ I have the right to be happy.

+ My Black body is deserving of love and touch.

+ I live my life as a model for others.

Badass to the Bone

"Anything is possible when you have the right people there to support you."

—**Misty Copeland**, American ballet dancer; she started ballet at the age of thirteen and made history as the first African American female principal dancer with the American Ballet Theatre

"We need mothers who are capable of being character builders, patient, loving, strong, and true, whose homes will be uplifting power in the race. This is one of the greatest needs of the hour."

—**Frances Ellen Watkins Harper**, abolitionist, poet, and activist; she published her first book of poems at the age of twenty-one

"We are not a problem people; we are a people with problems. We have historic strengths; we have survived because of family."

—**Dorothy Height**, a key figure in the American Civil Rights movement; she led the National Council of Negro Women and worked hard to further the rights of all African Americans

"My doctors told me I would never walk again. My mother told me I would. I believed my mother."

—**Wilma Rudolph**, American sprinter

"The greatness of a community is most accurately measured by the compassionate actions of its members."

—**Coretta Scott King**, American author, activist, and civil rights leader; a tomboy, she once accidentally cut a male cousin with an axe which led to Coretta's mother insisting she become more lady-like

"I'd like my grandchildren to be able to see that their grandmother stood up for something, a long time ago."

—**Claudette Colvin**, American civil rights activist and the first protester to not give up her bus seat for a white passenger; she was considered an inappropriate spokesperson for the bus boycott as an unwed teenage mother

"The women in your family have never lost touch with one another. Death is a path we take to meet on the other side."

—**Edwidge Danticat**, Haitian-American author; she defied her family's expectation that she work in medicine by pursuing a career in writing, and her first novel was an Oprah's Book Club pick

"The experience of poetry could bring my mother back to me. Poetry offers a different kind of solace—here on earth."

—**Natasha Trethewey**, American poet; she has often written about her experiences as a biracial woman living in the South

When Your Family Is Toxic

"It's not the load that breaks you down; it's the way you carry it."

—**Lena Horne**, American singer, dancer, actress, and civil rights activist; she
  became one of the first African American actors to sign a long-term contract
  with MGM

Because Black families were broken apart by the institution of slavery,
emancipation led to a tightening of bonds between family members.
Black families became stronger than they'd ever been in the past
and everyone in the family had a role to fulfill, whether it was the
youngest children, aunts and uncles, parents, or grandparents—even
the in-laws had a role. They all worked together to rebuild their
lives and lend support during rough times, whether it was financial,
physical, emotional, or psychological, and they all celebrated good
times together.

Unfortunately, many of us are not lucky enough to be part of an
all-loving family. Your parents might be fighting all the time. Maybe
they're selfish and indifferent. Maybe they're separated and you hate
the people they allow in their lives. Maybe you don't get along with
your siblings. Maybe you feel angry, anxious, helpless, or forced to
hide your emotions, and your self-esteem is very low.

Some family members have toxic behaviors, like manipulation,
aggression, or unkindness. The word "toxic" here describes behaviors
and not the person, because no one is 100 percent good, bad, or
toxic. All of us come with both positive qualities and our share of
flaws, and therefore it would be unfair to reduce a person, or a family,
to a single adjective. The word "toxic" refers to the behaviors that
people in the family might be displaying—behaviors that result in
concrete problems.

When people outside our home are being "toxic," we can choose to simply walk away. However, when the toxic individuals are our parents or siblings, the situation becomes much more complex.

If you're dealing (or have had to deal) with frightening and threatening events at home, you are more likely to suffer from academic problems, behavioral problems, and health problems. If you are being physically or emotionally abused or know someone who is being abused, you don't have to tolerate it. You can get help by speaking to a school counselor or talking to one of the counselors at the National Child Abuse Hotline. Their twenty-four-hour hotline number is 1-800-422-4453. If you don't feel comfortable making a call, they have a twenty-four-hour internet chat available with trained counselors at ChildHelp.org/hotline. Abuse can make you feel powerless and like you have no control over your life. And it can be scary to reach out for help, but if you are being hurt, you owe it to yourself to talk to someone who can give you some options that may make your life better.

Here are some signs that you're part of a toxic family:

You don't trust other people. If the toxic people in your life have used manipulation to control you, you might find that you no longer trust others—at home or outside of home—and that you have difficulty creating healthy relationships. Your guard is always up, and over time, getting rid of this constant state of alert seems to become more and more difficult.

Here are some examples of manipulation:

+ A toxic parent may use emotional blackmail to gain your affection; for instance, they may often speak badly about the other parent, trying to form an alliance against them.

+ A toxic parent may be passive aggressive. Instead of openly expressing how they are feeling, the person makes subtle comments to give you a guilt trip. Rather than clearly saying what's bothering them, they find petty ways to spite you until they get your attention.

When you can identify where the trust was broken and why this is an issue for you, then you can work on forgiving, healing, and establishing boundaries with a toxic family member.

You don't know what a healthy relationship looks like.
Our models of "love" are based on an inheritance of dysfunction passed down through slavery, oppression, racism, bigotry, and patriarchy. Our models of "love" are based on what Hollywood tells us is romantic. Physical and psychological violence, abuse, and neglect might distort your perception of what a caring relationship is even more. Subconsciously, you expect the people around you to overreact, be demanding, blame you, or abandon you. In many cases, we accept toxic behavior because we don't know any better! If you've always felt like you were walking on eggshells around your dad, you might not question a friendship where your best friend is always on the verge of yelling at you. Her toxicity will feel *familiar*.

Be Inspired:
Get to Know Tarana Burke

In 2006, Tarana Burke started the "Me Too" movement. She has worked tirelessly for decades as an advocate for survivors of sexual abuse, especially women of color. In 2017, inspired by Tarana's movement, the world saw a mobilization of the hashtag #MeToo, which led to a deeper understanding and awareness of the pervasiveness of sexual violence and the number of women who have survived sexual assaults; both well-known celebrities and private individuals shared their stories of surviving abuse, and called out for change.

"Me Too, in a lot of ways, is about agency. It's not about giving up your agency, it's about claiming it."

—**Tarana Burke**, American activist and a consultant on the Oscar-award-winning film *Selma* about the historic voting rights marches in Alabama

You don't know how to deal with stress. Our bodies respond to extreme stress by triggering a "flight or fight" response wherein a flood of stress hormone—called cortisol—is released into the body, signaling to the brain that it's time to either flee or stand your ground and fight. The hormones have several effects that help the body survive an attack: our heart rate increases, blood pressure rises, and we begin to breathe faster. This dilates our blood vessels and the air passages in our lungs, which sends more oxygen to our vital organs and brain. Our senses sharpen. While under the duress of stress, we remain on high alert, and the reasoning and memory centers of our brains are less active, so our attention becomes more focused on either fighting the danger or running away from it.

If you're constantly in a stressful situation at home, with frightening or threatening situations occurring too frequently, stress becomes chronic and disrupts the brain's and body's responses. High levels of stress have been linked to many different medical conditions like autoimmune disorders, high blood pressure, and mental illnesses. How do you know if you are under chronic stress?

You feel like a small kid. Toxic family members refuse to acknowledge that you have a mind of your own. They treat you like a helpless little thing. They want to control and command you, and if they meet even a little resistance, they become upset and make you feel guilty. You're not allowed to make your own decisions, your privacy is constantly violated, and you lack any kind of independence. You're anxious all the time, afraid to do something new, and unable to fit in. You do not feel listened to or respected and develop low self-esteem or even inappropriate behaviors.

You don't know who you are because you're not given the chance to build your own identity. As a result, you may suffer from anxiety attacks and depression. Because of your low self-esteem, you criticize yourself a lot; you feel stupid, worthless, and not deserving of anything better. You come to accept the idea that you are "less" than others.

Sometimes, the opposite happens. Instead of feeling like a small kid, you feel like the adult in the family. One or even both parents are very immature on all levels. Their weak sense of responsibility, their lack of interest, their carelessness or poor control of their impulses make them unreliable. You're forced to take on adult responsibilities and grow up too fast, which is neither appropriate nor healthy.

You ignore your emotions. Maybe you've never learned to properly express your feelings, because the "wrong" words could lead to serious abuse from one of your parents. So you hide your pain, your resentment, your anger. Maybe you find yourself prioritizing other people's emotions over your own. If you ignore your emotions, it might be difficult for you to know who you are, how you feel, and what you want in life. You're held back by your doubts and your inability to relate to other people.

Sometimes, the emotional distance that exists within your family might not be obvious to those looking from the outside. Some parents meet the primary needs of their children: the family never runs out of food, books, or even fun vacations. But behind the façade, these individuals are cold: no hugs, no kisses, no signs of affection, no support, no understanding. As a teenager, you might find that you're self-sufficient but lack the ability to connect with others on an emotional level. Maybe you don't feel worthy of affection and harbor feelings of inferiority.

You can't stand failure. If you're in a toxic environment at home, you might constantly feel inadequate and unworthy. Your parents might have asked too much of you, without ever showing gratitude or satisfaction. And here you are now—with low self-esteem and an unquenchable thirst for attention, on the verge of an anxiety attack at the very idea of failure. You often feel anxious and insecure. You may have difficulty concentrating. You're irritable, hyperactive, worried, and tense.

Toxic families are full of conflict, abuse of authority, and dysfunctional dynamics that affect all their members. Because of their personalities, their behaviors, or their ways of communicating, toxic parents hurt or destroy emotional balance, motivation, and self-esteem. This constantly creates an atmosphere full of tension, skin-deep emotions, and high levels of anxiety.

 **Affirmations Station**

+ I am able to say no without being afraid of displeasing.

+ I erase from my life all the people who prevent me from achieving happiness.

+ My life matters.

+ I deserve a fulfilled life.

+ I deserve respect and attention.

+ I choose to cleanse myself of my fears and doubts.

Badass to the Bone

"Oh, Misery, I have drunk thy cup of sorrow to its dregs, but I am still a rebel."

—**Lucy Parsons**, American labor organizer and radical socialist; she founded the Industrial Workers of the World and was an outspoken activist focusing on women, people of color, and the disenfranchised

"You can't focus on the bad thing; you have to focus on getting through it."

—**Ciara**, American singer, songwriter, dancer, and model; an entrepreneur, she has taken seminars at Harvard Business School and is part owner of the Seattle Sounders MLS team

"Never underestimate the power of dreams and the influence of the human spirit. We are all the same in this notion. The potential for greatness lives within each of us."

—**Wilma Rudolph**, American sprinter

"Hard days are the best because that's when champions are made."

—**Gabby Douglas**, American artistic gymnast; she once took a two-year break from competitive gymnastics—we love a self-care queen who takes breaks

"Those parts of yourself that you desperately want to hide and destroy will gain power over you. The best thing to do is face and own them, because they are forever a part of you."

—**Janet Mock**, American writer, television host, director, producer, and transgender rights activist; she began her writing career at *People* magazine

"Sometimes you've got to let everything go—purge yourself. If you are unhappy with anything…whatever is bringing you down, get rid of it. Because you'll find that when you're free, your true creativity, your true self comes out."

—**Tina Turner**, American-born Swiss singer, songwriter, dancer, and actress

"I have been in Sorrow's kitchen and licked out all the pots. Then I have stood on the peaky mountain wrapped in rainbows, with a harp and a sword in my hands."

—**Zora Neale Hurston**, American author, anthropologist, and filmmaker

"The more you praise and celebrate your life, the more there is in life to celebrate."

—**Oprah Winfrey**, American talk show host, actress, television producer, media executive, and philanthropist

What Can You Do?

"You must never be fearful about what you are doing when it is right."

—**Rosa Parks**, American activist

No one deserves to live in an emotionally toxic environment. Some malicious, intrusive, or violent behaviors and words have lasting, harmful consequences. But what can you do? You might feel that you're stuck, with no way out.

Define the situation. If it sometimes gets violent, making sure that you are physically safe has to be your number one priority. Have a list ready of places you can go in an emergency situation. Pick people you know will protect you until the crisis passes—like very close friends or relatives. If you don't have anyone available to help you, go to a public place where other people will see you and where you feel safe. If you are physically injured and need help right away, go to a fire station or to a police station. Explain the situation at home to the people you go to.

+ If you cannot leave your house and your parents are being abusive, try to go to your room and lock the door.

+ If you are in immediate danger and cannot leave the house, try to find a safe place within the house. Lock yourself in a bathroom, for instance, somewhere where you are protected. Call Emergency Services for help. If you don't have a phone handy, scream and holler for help.

+ If you are able to get out of the house, but don't know where to go, head for the closest fire or police station.

Remember, you're not at fault. Use the toxic attacks from your family member as an opportunity to practice the art of not taking things too personally. If you can master it in this relationship, then it will be much easier for you to apply the skills as well in your interactions with others outside the family. Family members with toxic behavior patterns will probably try to imply that you did something wrong and give you a guilt trip, trying to destroy your confidence and destabilize your resolve. Remember, there is enormous freedom that comes from knowing that you're not to blame—even when the person with toxic behaviors tries to make you feel that you are.

Talk about it. When you feel ready, approach the abusive family member and confidently (nonaggressively) communicate to them how upset you are about the way they behave. The goal here is not necessarily to change their behavior, because, after all, only they can control what they do. The idea is to change your reaction. You're no longer pretending that everything is fine, that you're okay having

this person walk all over you. You're showing your strength and
letting them know that you are very aware that their behavior is
inappropriate. If the abusive family member cannot be reasoned with,
seek support. It is important to get help—either from a counselor at
school or from a therapist who can help you resolve both relationship
conflicts and individual conflicts. Sometimes, you might have to
involve law enforcement, particularly if your life is in danger. In
any case, *find an adult you can trust* to be open with. Many times in
situations like this, you might feel scared or ashamed. But if you are
afraid of your parents, that's a big red flag that you need to get help.
Remember, this isn't your fault. You didn't do anything wrong, and
it's not wrong to protect yourself. And keep trying to find people who
can help you if the first adult you talk to is unwilling to intervene. Try
a teacher, a school counselor, the school nurse, a doctor, friends of the
family, other people in your family you can trust. *Don't stop telling until
you get the help you deserve and need.*

Distance yourself from the abusive individual. Someone
once said it, and it is often repeated: "Avoid negative people, they
always have a problem for every solution." Distancing yourself
doesn't necessarily mean burning bridges, but it's okay if you need
your own space for a while. You're not being an ungrateful child,
sister, grandchild, niece, cousin, etc. On the contrary, you're being
thoughtful by avoiding the drama or avoiding all interactions with
someone who constantly criticizes you, gets on your nerves, provokes
you, disrespects you, and puts you down. It is your right to remove
yourself from a painful situation and search for serenity.

It's important to set boundaries. As you grow older, you
have more say in how much contact you need to have with violent
relatives; you have more independence and more flexibility in
determining what (if any) relationship you want to have with people
who behave in toxic ways. For one thing, you have the ability to set
boundaries with others and let go of connections that aren't loving

and bringing you greater joy. In order to protect yourself, you may need to set boundaries right now with people in your life, regardless of what stage of life you are at. To do so, remember: be clear and direct. Get right to the point. Speak in statements that begin with "I" not "you." Tell the person what you are experiencing, why you are setting the boundary, and exactly what the boundary is. For example, "I don't like how I feel when you call me names, and I'm not going to tolerate it any longer. I won't be spending time with you from now on." If the conversation turns violent or becomes abusive in any way, simply say, "I expect to be treated with respect. We're done talking. Goodbye."

Practice self-care. Surrounding yourself with positive people is the key to staying confident when dealing with an abusive family member who demeans or humiliates you. This is especially true if the abuse comes from a parent. Very often, friends will show you the respect and appreciation that family never afforded you. Chosen carefully, friends will help restore your dignity and your happiness. If you are forced to live or work with an abusive person, then make sure you get enough time alone to rest and recover. Having to be Zen in the face of toxic mood swings can be exhausting, and, if you're not careful, the toxicity can infect you. Abusive family members can keep you awake by causing you to constantly question yourself: "Am I doing the right thing? Am I really so terrible that they despise me so much? Why don't they agree with my life choices?" Thoughts like these can keep you in a stressful situation for weeks, months, or even years. Sometimes this is the goal of an abusive family member: to put you in a state of anguish. And since you can't control everything they do, it's important to take care of yourself so that you can stay focused on your health and be prepared to live positively. Practicing meditation on a regular basis is one beneficial exercise.

Distract yourself. Living with violent family members can pose many challenges, including not being able to leave the house when things get rough. It may help to isolate yourself away from the fighting and distract yourself behind a closed door—at least until you are able to find someone you can talk to. This can be beneficial if your parents are verbally abusive to you or others in your family. Some of the following activities may help you distract yourself during a crisis if you are not in immediate danger.

+ Write about what you're experiencing in a journal. Writing will allow you to release your pent-up emotions and preserve your mental health. Your journal is the one place you can say whatever you feel like saying without any fears or retribution. Keep your journal in a safe place.

+ Try soothing white noise like waves crashing on a beach or rainforest sounds. This will counter the upsetting sounds of fighting and yelling. Or put on some headphones and listen to your favorite music.

+ Find an activity you enjoy like drawing, painting, watching a movie, or reading a book. Even if it just gives you a short break from the chaos, it's worth it to step aside and engage in something you enjoy doing.

Forgive, but don't forget. Let go of your desire for payback; regardless of how despicably a family member has acted, never let hatred take hold in your heart. Fighting hate with hate will hurt you more. When you decide to hate someone, you automatically start digging two graves: one for your enemy and one for you. Hateful grudges can destroy your life and those around you. Forgiveness gives you the strength to move on to something more beneficial for you, something you love. After all, the best revenge is to be the opposite of the person who hurt you. The best revenge is to be very positively alive, in a way that creates peace in your heart.

Forgive. It is important to forgive in order to free yourself. In a way it's a selfish act. Forgiveness is necessary for your own progress. You have to understand this: abusive people will not change overnight; there is no point in deluding yourself. However, it is possible to detach yourself from the destructive power they have over you. An abusive parent might have caused your inner turmoil, but you're responsible for the attitude adjustment that will allow you to overcome the abuse.

Sometimes, you just have to let it go. Yes, people can change, and some toxic family relationships can be repaired, but only if both people involved are ready to do the necessary work. It's hard and painful work, especially if you believe that trust cannot be restored. Unfortunately, sometimes all you can do is just let go. This is your life—and you have the right to walk away. No explanation needed. You don't have justify your decision…to anybody.

Affirmations Station

Affirmations adapted from the words of Audre Lorde, Issa Rae, Iyanla Vanzant, Oprah Winfrey, and First Lady Michelle Obama.

+ I face my fears. Because I am fierce. Because I am Black. Because I am a badass Black girl.

+ I dare to be powerful; I dare to use my strength in the service of my vision.

+ I thrive on obstacles. If I'm told that I can't, I push harder.

+ I find the people who make me better.

+ I'm willing to look at my darkness because it empowers me to change.

Badass to the Bone

"If you don't live your life, then who will?"

—**Rihanna**, Barbadian singer, songwriter, actress, businesswoman, and philanthropist

"Don't let anyone rob you of your imagination, your creativity, or your curiosity. It's your place in the world; it's your life. Go on and do all you can with it, and make it the life you want to live."

—**Mae Jemison**, American engineer, physician, and former NASA astronaut

"I gave myself permission to feel and experience all of my emotions. In order to do that, I had to stop being afraid to feel. In order to do that, I taught myself to believe that no matter what I felt or what happened when I felt it, I would be okay."

—**Iyanla Vanzant**, American inspirational speaker, lawyer, New Thought spiritual teacher, author, life coach, and television personality

"Hate is too great a burden to bear. It injures the hater more than it injures the hated."

—**Coretta Scott King**, American author, activist, civil rights leader, and the wife of Martin Luther King Jr.

"My skin absorbs the sun's rays and my hair defies gravity. You can't tell me I'm not magical."

—**Unknown**

"I am a strong woman with or without this other person, with or without this job, and with or without these tight pants."

—**Queen Latifah**, American rapper, singer, songwriter, actress, and producer; she was a key player in reshaping the rap industry to make space for women rappers

"You have a color of your own—Dark chocolate,
You have a culture of your own—Hip pop,
You have a revival of your own—Harlem Renaissance,
You are the spot on a ladybug that adds its beauty,
You are the pupil of an eye,
You are the vastness of space,
You are the richness of soil,
You are the sweetness of dark chocolate,
You are the mystery in nature,
Blessed Black chocolate, God has made You to rule the Land that made You a slave."

—**Luffina Lourduraj**, poet; she notes the sacrificial love of mothers, saying, "She sacrifices her dreams to make my dream come true"

Ode to Friendship: The Family We Choose

"If we treated ourselves as well as we treated our best friend, can you imagine?"

—**Meghan Markle**, American-born Duchess of Sussex and advocate for women's rights and social justice; she shook up the British royal family lineage just by marrying into it

Friends can be just like family—only we get to choose them! Even
without the blood ties that naturally unite us with our brothers and
sisters, bonds of friendship—sometimes even stronger than family
ones—can unite us with people who become so close to us that they
are considered family, whether it's the big brother we didn't have or
the little sister we would have liked to have.

Whether it's a childhood friend we met in the neighborhood sandbox,
a friend from elementary school with whom we played Marco Polo in
the park, a friend from high school with whom we have forged bonds
during the trying period of adolescence, or even a work colleague with
whom we become very close, all friendships feed us. No matter how
they came into being, they all had a reason to establish themselves
and, at times, to crumble. Each friendship is unique and has a unique
dynamic. There are billions of friendly affiliations on the planet,
and none are the same: that's the beauty of it. We must enjoy the
good times shared, not forget the lessons learned the hard way, and,
above all, understand that each person who enters our life does so
for a reason that only fate knows, and it is up to us to understand
the meaning.

Take time to nurture your most valued friendships the way you
would nurture any living thing. Even if it's the kind of friendship
where you can go years without talking and pick up as if you never
spent a day apart, be more vigilant and protective of these kinds of
connections because they are life-affirming and enriching. Write a
letter to your friend, buy them a cookie, or surprise them with flowers
you picked from a field. Anything you do to nourish these bonds is
worth the growth you'll gain from having a close friend who has your
back and knows you well enough to be honest with you, even if it's
sometimes difficult.

Affirmations Station

Affirmations adapted from the words of Beyoncé, Oprah, Maya Angelou, and Janelle Monáe.

+ I have the power to inspire and empower.

+ I see my flaws, but also the true beauty and strength that's inside of me.

+ Passion is the log that keeps the fire of my purpose blazing.

+ If I don't like something, I change it. If I can't change it, I change my attitude.

+ I inspire others to feel stronger, braver, and more beautiful inside and out.

+ I own my superpower and use my strength to change the world around me.

Badass to the Bone

"If I don't have friends, then I ain't got nothin'."

—**Billie Holiday**, American jazz and swing music singer

"It seems to me that trying to live without friends is like milking a bear to get cream for your morning coffee. It is a whole lot of trouble, and then not worth much after you get it."

—**Zora Neale Hurston**, American author, anthropologist, and filmmaker

"The success of every woman should be the inspiration to another. We should raise each other up. Make sure you're very courageous: be strong, be extremely kind, and above all be humble."

—**Serena Williams**, American professional tennis player

"Friendship between women can resemble love. It has the same possessiveness as love, the same jealousies and lack of restraint. But the complicities of friendship are more durable than those of love, for they are not based on the language of the body."

—**Maryse Condé**, Guadeloupean novelist, critic, and playwright

"A lot of women, when they're young, feel they have very good friends, and find later on that friendship is complicated. It's easy to be friends when everyone's eighteen. It gets harder the older you get, as you make different life choices, as people say in America. A lot of women's friendships begin to founder. I was interested in why that was, why it's not possible for a woman to see her friend living differently and just think, Oh, she lives differently."

—**Zadie Smith**, English novelist, essayist, and short-story writer of Jamaican descent

"If friends disappoint you over and over, that's in large part your own fault. Once someone has shown a tendency to be self-centered, you need to recognize that and take care of yourself; people aren't going to change simply because you want them to."

—**Oprah Winfrey**, American talk show host, actress, television producer, media executive, and philanthropist

"Abandon the cultural myth that all female friendships must be bitchy, toxic, or competitive. This myth is like heels and purses—pretty but designed to SLOW women down."

—**Roxane Gay**, American writer, professor, editor, and social commentator; her work focuses on the analysis and deconstruction of feminist and racial issues

"Friendship takes work. Finding friends, nurturing friendships, scheduling face time, it all takes a tremendous amount of work. But it's worth it. If you put in the effort, you'll see the rewards of positive friends who will make your life extraordinary."

—**Maya Angelou**, American poet, memoirist, and civil rights activist

Remember, no matter how wonderful your friends or family are (or how horrible they can be as well), you are already your own best friend. Over the course of your life, people will come, some will stay, some will wander away or leave suddenly and inexplicably, and through all of that, you always have *you*. They say that hindsight is twenty-twenty, and thirty or forty years from now the people you think are most important in your life may still be as important, but, chances are, you will be the one constant you can depend on.

If you are going through a rough period in your life right now, remember that's subject to change as well. Things get better if you are mindful and take the steps to get yourself into a better situation. And have some faith in yourself. You're stuck with you for the rest of your life. You may as well believe in yourself.

CHAPTER SIX

....

Resilience in the Face of Challenge

"Activism is my rent for living on the planet."

—**Alice Walker**, American novelist, short-story writer, poet, and social activist

An activist is someone who sees the need for change and devotes their time to doing something about it. They commit to protest and resist what they perceive as injustice. Those who don't see the point in becoming activists live in a space of privilege where they see no need for a change in the world or are apathetic or unaware of injustice. They probably did not suffer the kind of discrimination or abuse that would push them to defend civil rights and dismantle systems of economic, social, and political oppression.

Being an activist can mean a lot of things, including working full time at an organization or dedicating a large chunk of your free time to a cause. It is as much a calling as it is a profession. You see something wrong in the world, and you try to change it.

Anyone can be an activist. Men can fight for feminist causes. White people can help fight racism. There's no set model of what an activist looks like, and little protests can yield big results. Greta Thunberg started a global climate change awareness movement by sitting outside of Swedish Parliament with a sign. Ghandi went on hunger strikes. Rosa Parks simply refused to change her seat on a public bus. Whatever unique vision you bring to activism will only enrich it and make the group you join (or start) stronger and add a valued perspective.

If you want to be an activist, start with affirmations for nonviolence toward yourself:

✦ Today, I am at peace with myself.

✦ Today, I forgive myself.

✦ Today, I practice self-compassion.

✦ Today, I live in the present moment and release the past.

✦ Today, I choose to be aware of what I talk about, and I refuse to gossip.

Choosing a Cause

"I was a person with dignity and self-respect, and I should not set my sights lower than anybody else just because I was Black."

—**Rosa Parks**, American activist

"Keep trying. Don't give up. Every presentation at a conference, every article and book published means incremental change."

—**Rev. Dr. Dianne Glave**, environmental historian and theologian; she is adamant about bringing African Americans into the conversation concerning the history of the environment

If you want to become an activist, how do you choose a cause? From climate change to mass incarceration, income inequality

to homelessness, trying to focus your attention on one issue can
be overwhelming.

Here's some advice:

Get personal. There are many great causes out there, but find
something that is a match for your own history and values. Find
something that aligns with what you're passionate about; this will
keep you engaged and allow you to better contribute. You may be
wondering, "How do I choose just one cause? And what if I choose
wrong?" It may feel like if you pick one cause to support, then
somehow, you're leaving the others behind. But you cannot change
everything. Choose carefully. Develop a personal mission statement,
and then identify causes that resonate with that mission. Ask yourself
what's most important to you in life. What do you want your life
to center around? What doesn't feel like work to you? How do you
want others to perceive you? What kind of legacy do you want to
leave future generations? Don't feel like you need to limit yourself.
Dream big. Your mission statement might be something like: "I want
to spread the message that conservation can save us from global
warming." Find causes that ignite your passion and donate and/or
participate. Which organizations or causes do you feel most drawn to?
If you have friends or people you admire who do "give-back" work,
what do they do? Is there something you've been curious about but
never tried, like walking shelter dogs? Try out a few things and see
what gets you fired up.

Cherno Biko uses Twitter hashtags like #FolksLikeUs and
#BlackTransLifesMatter to raise awareness about the violence trans women
of color face.

Writer, filmmaker, and activist **Bree Newsome** climbed to the top
of the flagpole in front of South Carolina's state house to protest the
Confederate flag.

Beverly Bond founded Black Girls Rock, Inc., an organization that aims to empower Black girls. She tweets about Black women who are leaders and innovators and uses her timeline to publicize leadership events for Black women.

Alicia Garza, one of the founders of Black Lives Matter, tweets about BLM and is also a source of information about trans rights and global freedom struggles.

Johnetta Elzie created WeTheProtesters.org and helped found Campaign Zero, which aims to reform the criminal justice system in the United States. She is also involved in Black Lives Matter and helped organize protests in Ferguson after Mike Brown was killed.

Activist and author **J. Skyler** tweets about racism, feminist issues, and ignorance in pop culture, along with the politics of sexuality.

Pace yourself. Before you join a group, ask questions and weigh your options. Make sure the organization's philosophy is in line with your own. For example, if you are a vegan, does the organization take donations from meat producers? If someone tries to pressure you into joining a cause, especially one you aren't committed to, or tries to lay on a guilt trip, walk away.

Go local. Consider joining the efforts of a local organization tackling a local problem. Maybe your library has a program to increase adult literacy and needs volunteers. Donating time is often the best heart warmer. It feels great to have the chance to give back to the community and to be a part of something bigger than yourself. What give-back opportunities are available in your community? Are there any you could spearhead yourself?

Research. There's a difference between wanting to help and knowing you need to be a part of the solution, and research is one of the quickest ways to get clear on where you stand. Learn about American history and develop a functional understanding of how government works. Develop strong arguments to back up your positions. Two very effective ways to do this include familiarizing yourself with arguments used by people with whom you agree, as well as with arguments used by people with whom you disagree. For example, do you know the platform of those who are opposed to defunding the police? Follow the news. Search the internet for blogs that focus on your topic. Read newspapers and follow the evening news for questions you might not even have thought of yet, questions that are just starting to reach a boiling point. Learn how to tell a credible source from propaganda.

Commit for the long run. No matter which cause you select, your activism path will most likely be more about the journey than the destination. Do you think you can devote your time and energy to this cause (or do you think you would burn out quickly)? Do you have a passion for this? If you feel that you can answer yes to these questions, it proves you at least have the drive to participate. The famous "I can't believe we still have to protest this s*&@" sign from the #MeToo marches indicates the longevity of some causes, as well as the fact that certain issues may never be fully resolved. Are you willing to maintain hope? You will certainly experience depressing setbacks, but activist movements take time.

Join a group. Activists don't work well alone, and those who try usually burn out pretty quickly. Your best bet is to join a group that focuses on your concern. Interested in animal rights? Think about joining the Humane Society. Attend meetings. Networking with other activists will educate you, provide you with a support network, and help you focus your energies on productive activism strategies.

Stay centered. Don't hate people you don't agree with. If you forget how to communicate with people on the other side of the issue, you will lose your ability to sway others toward your position. Remember to practice self-care; it will take you further in getting others to join your cause. It is important to take care of yourself, so if you feel like you need to step back for a bit or try a different way to help within your group, then do so. It's okay to step back from protests to stuff envelopes for a few months if you're growing tired.

Get a degree—it will open doors that may otherwise remain closed to you. A law degree is an ambitious goal, but lawyers are trained in the necessary skills to tackle broad platforms at the government level. Even graduating with a bachelor's degree in law or a social science can be extremely helpful, and nothing says you can't pursue your cause or causes while you are in school. Many famous activists have done this, like Thurgood Marshall and Nelson Mandela.

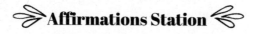

Affirmations Station

+ Today, I create a ripple of kindness throughout the world.

+ Today, I greet everyone with compassion and respect.

+ Today, I view people as they present themselves, without stereotype or prejudice.

+ Today, I learn something new about a different culture than my own.

+ Today, I am thankful for my challenges because they lead me toward healing.

+ Today, I affirm that all living beings are my family members!

What You Can Do

"We will not let the colonizers rob us of our right to belong to the earth and to have agency in the food system. We are Black gold—our melanin-rich skin the mirror of the sacred soil in all her hues. We belong here, bare feet planted firmly on the land, hands calloused with the work of sustaining and nourishing our community."

—**Leah Penniman**, farmer and activist; Through Soul Fire Farm, she has inspired and educated diverse communities about farming, using her influence to improve conditions for Black and other minority farmers

If you don't know where to start on your journey as an activist, here are some pointers:

1. **Take part in debates on public policy issues.** Don't hesitate to let your voice be heard when a public issue arises. Do not say to yourself, "This does not concern me. Nothing will change anyway." It only takes five minutes to convey to a person that communitarianism and tribalism are dangerous for our societies or why education for all is an essential condition for sustainable development. With education for example, limiting who can go to school or into training programs keeps one group of people in a lower socioeconomic group and breeds ignorance, which leads to a slew of other problems like crime and racial disharmony. It is also possible for you to realize the limit of your arguments during these discussions. Some people are so entrenched in their own thought patterns that they can't be reached no matter what you say or do. If that happens, try asking questions. It's also possible that you might realize that your opinion is wrong. You may not have a complete understanding of why someone believes what they believe. That's okay. You should never stop learning. Talk, but also take the time to listen.

2. **Take care of the most vulnerable.** Imagine being at a school or in an office where a person in a wheelchair

cannot access the bathroom because of the narrow hallway leading to it. Are you going to say to yourself, "Well, I have access, so everything is cool!" Or are you going to take it to administration? If you go for number two, congratulations! You've got what it takes to be an activist. The aim here is of course to empower others to be independent and have equal access. Don't make the mistake of feeling sorry for anyone, because then you run the risk of missing out on their gifts.

3. **Stay informed.** Knowing all the facts allows you to clearly analyze a situation, understand your rights and the loopholes that exist in the system, and above all to recognize candidates who actually care about your cause. Educate those around you in digestible, accessible language so that they too understand their rights. Creating a blog is a great way to share ideas and inspire others, especially if you are disconnected geographically from the movements that interest you. One of the great things about the internet is that it opens access to parts of the world that used to be closed off due to distance. Spend some time learning about the political situation globally, especially if it ties into your own interests. If you are an anti-racist, for example, learn about the political situation in places with a history of racism or current problems with ethnic cleansing. Learning about the history in South Africa, Sudan, or Rwanda might help you better understand the situation in the United States and what exactly is at stake.

4. **Promote your rights, but also do your civic duties.** Rights and civic duties ultimately have the same goal—the preservation of a peaceful society in which everyone enjoys a standard and pleasant living environment. So don't just claim your rights—doing your civic duties is just as important. Vote if you are eligible. Join a voter registration drive or fight for voting rights for those who are disenfranchised. Volunteer at a polling place on Election Day. Learn about the political process. But also remember civic duty goes beyond politics. It's

about making sure your community is thriving by doing your part, even if it's something practical like picking up litter.

5. **Adopt good habits.** Good habits can be very simple, especially in the case of environmental protection: do not leave the light on unnecessarily so as not to waste energy, don't leave the water running, avoid the use of pesticides, support organic farmers, or choose to walk or bike instead of driving. Environmental justice is also racial justice. Think of the situation in Flint, Michigan, with its polluted water: who was impacted? In the 1970s, there were many instances of pollution that were directly tied to the economic and racial demographic of the people whose land, water, and air were being polluted. Be vocal about clean water and air pollution, because it is essential to quality-of-life issues.

6. **Follow the rules.** Do not encroach on the rights of others. Respect for traffic lights, for example, aims to preserve human life. Respecting the law not only shows that you're concerned about your fellow citizens and your environment, it also helps you not to practice what you denounce. The abuses of our leaders are due to the fact that they do not respect the laws; they believe they are above them. Respect for the law may also keep you safe, although it certainly doesn't guarantee you won't be hassled by someone in law enforcement (or worse, brutalized). It does take away the ammunition of those who believe law enforcement is entitled to behave without criticism.

7. **Disconnect.** Our professional and recreational activities increasingly require an almost permanent presence on the internet. This virtual world sometimes leads us to forget the real world and the worries that go with it, whether they are our own or those of our loved ones. We talked about volunteering your time for causes you care about: give time to those who love you and who you love first. Be there for your family and friends, give them your focus, listen to them, and participate

in their development. Sometimes just having your undivided attention is worth more than anything else to them.

Affirmations Station

- ✦ I will respect and be mindful of other drivers on the road and treat them with kindness and patience.

- ✦ I will respect the elderly and treat them with dignity today and always.

- ✦ I will be a role model to any children I encounter and treat them with care.

- ✦ I will listen with an open heart to at least one person today.

- ✦ I will bring peace into my home and treat my family with love and kindness.

Badass to the Bone

"You don't make progress by standing on the sidelines, whimpering and complaining. You make progress by implementing ideas."

—**Shirley Chisholm**, American politician, educator, and author; she was the first African American woman in congress and the first to make a bid for the US Presidency

"You can never know where you are going unless you know where you have been."

—**Amelia Boynton Robinson**, leader of the civil rights movement in Selma; she started campaigning for women's suffrage in the 1920s and, after being beaten during a march, Amelia refused to quit

"It's not about color. It's about love."

—**Unknown**

"The African race is a rubber ball. The harder you dash it to the ground, the higher it will rise."

—**African proverb**

"Defining myself, as opposed to being defined by others, is one of the most difficult challenges I face."

—**Carol Moseley-Braun**, the first female African American senator; she ran for congress because she felt politicians were out of touch with everyday Americans

"There are times in life when, instead of complaining, you do something about your complaints."

—**Rita Dove**, American poet and essayist; in 1993 she was the first African American to be named US poet laureate

"The most common way people give up their power is by thinking they don't have any."

—**Alice Walker**, American novelist, short-story writer, poet, and social activist

"I've had to learn to fight all my life—got to learn to keep smiling. If you smile, things will work out."

—**Serena Williams**, American professional tennis player

"Caring for myself is not self-indulgence, it is self-preservation, and that is an act of political warfare."

—**Audre Lorde**, American author and activist

Fight Against Racism

A lot of people of color are tired—tired of being unseen and misunderstood. It's important for everyone, regardless of race, to ask, "What is my role in this system?" and then do everything possible to dismantle it, starting within ourselves.

Here are some ways to fight against racism:

1. **Get comfortable saying, "That's racist."** Think of it as an observation with no judgment on the person or item in question. If you think about it, we're all part of a racist system; it's all around us. You'll be pointing out the obvious that many people miss.

2. **Use your social media for good.** Share useful information on your social media pages. Social media is also a good place to have meaningful discussions. During times of crisis, like during widespread protests, social media can be the best source of information on what is happening on the ground.

3. **Seek out, learn from, and amplify other Black voices.** For most of recorded history, the amplified voices have been white. One of the simplest ways to fight racism is to start amplifying Black voices and listening to Black leaders.

4. **Pressure leaders to end police violence.** Write or call your representatives. Start a petition. Support candidates for sheriff positions who are willing to look at alternatives to traditional policing.

5. **Attend protests.** Especially if you've never been to one. Protests can be great sources of inspiration for new and emerging activists.

6. **Record questionable interactions.** If you see an interaction that looks like it may go awry, use your cell phone

to capture video/audio of the encounter, especially if it's between police and a Black person. The more these events are recorded and disseminated, the less likely police will be to step out of line.

7. **Believe survivors of racism.** It's hard to believe that anyone could doubt racist reports, but it happens. If someone tells you they've been through a racist encounter, see how you can help them. And believe them.

8. **Interrogate biases.** Stop talking and start listening in order to validate others' feelings and emotions. But question biases— other people's and your own. Sometimes, in the process of opening up, you'll uncover hidden biases you weren't aware of, and you'll discover plenty in other people. Always question authority.

9. **Bring other Black people into positions of power.** The only way racism is going to be dismantled is if Black people are empowered. When you hear someone speaking truth, gather attention to what they are saying. Hush the crowd. Give them space and a platform to speak. Suggest people you know would do a good job for positions of authority. Let them know they have your support. Otherwise, it's just lip service.

10. **Use your voice to change policies in your community.** If you don't speak up and do something, who will? Attend town hall and city council meetings and speak if you have the opportunity. Start a blog about your community. Be vocal about the local issues, because they're often representative of larger systemic patterns.

11. **Give your time.** If you're looking for a way to get started, check out the many national civil rights organizations, and sign up to become a tutor or a mentor in an organization that empowers Black people.

12. **Donate money.** Or start a fundraising campaign if you don't have a lot of money to give. Every little bit helps.

13. **Speak up by using your creative talents.** On social media, there are many examples of artists, from painters to jewelry makers, selling their wares and giving proceeds to an organization pushing for change.

14. **Practice self-care.** Fighting racism can wear you out. Make sure you take the time to recharge and refocus your energy.

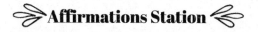

Affirmations Station

✦ I pray for peace for all the countries of the world and that their leaders act with love.

✦ I acknowledge every person's inalienable rights to life, liberty, and the pursuit of happiness on equal terms.

✦ I dedicate myself to a world vision greater than my meager needs.

✦ Today, I will honor and celebrate what peace there is in the world.

✦ Today, I honor my relationships by practicing peace in my communications and interactions.

Badass to the Bone

"When my brothers try to draw a circle to exclude me, I shall draw a larger circle to include them. Where they speak out for the privileges of a puny group, I shall shout for the rights of all mankind."

—**Pauli Murray**, lawyer and civil rights activist; two decades before the 1960s civil rights movement, she refused to move to the back of the bus in Virginia

"In a racist society, it is not enough to be non-racist. We must be anti-racist."

—**Dr. Angela Davis**, American political activist, philosopher, academic, and author

"The very serious function of racism is distraction. It keeps you from doing your work. It keeps you explaining, over and over again, your reason for being."

—**Toni Morrison**, American novelist, essayist, book editor, and college professor

"As long as you keep a person down, some part of you has to be down there to hold the person down, so it means you cannot soar as you otherwise might."

—**Marian Anderson**, American opera singer; the first African American to perform at the Metropolitan Opera in New York City, she went from singing on the street to singing at the request of President Roosevelt

"The beauty of anti-racism is that you don't have to pretend to be free of racism to be an anti-racist. Anti-racism is the commitment to fight racism wherever you find it, including in yourself. And it's the only way forward."

—**Ijeoma Oluo**, Nigerian-American writer on race, social justice, mental health, entertainment and the tech industry; she believes that publishing online allows you to decide your own professional course

"I wanted the young African American girls also on the bus to know that they had a right to be there, because they had paid their fare just like the white passengers."

—**Claudette Colvin**, American civil rights activist

"Freedom without the means to be self-supporting is a one-armed triumph."

—**Michelle Cliff**, Jamaican-American poet and author; a light-skinned Black lesbian, her poetry and fiction focused on the effects of post-colonialism on multi-cultural identity

Fight for Environmental and Climate Justice

"There are still many causes worth sacrificing for, so much history yet to be made."

—**Michelle Obama**, American attorney, author, and former First Lady of the United States

"Having been born during the colonial era where my family and a lot of my relatives were organizing against the colonial regime, where the liberation movement was extremely active and mobilizing, I later grew up to understand that people must organize and build movements against injustice."

—**Melanie Chiponda**, Johannesburg-based organizer; she quit her government job to focus on fighting for human rights in her country

The climate crisis is getting a lot of attention recently. The global temperature has risen by more than 1.6 degrees Fahrenheit since 1906, and our polar ice caps are rapidly melting. But there's more to the crisis than just warmer weather. Climate change is also changing weather patterns around the globe, increasing the frequency of wildfires, causing sea levels to rise, and wreaking havoc on marine animals as well as those who live on land. Young protestors have created one of the most dynamic movements in recent history and are reaching politicians in a way few protesters do. There are many opportunities to lend your support to this movement in a way that is meaningful to you, from helping set up a local composting program to canvassing for climate-focused political candidates. Remember that issues of the environment are often tied to issues of race and poverty. Poorer and/or Blacker communities have less protections and tend to live in more congested urban areas where pollution is rampant. And when a poor area is affected by pollution as we saw in Flint, Michigan, the residents have fewer resources to fight for environmental justice. Write down the issues you care about most—building renewable energy systems, banning single-use plastic, building resilience in frontline communities—and choose what you want to focus on.

Then, inform yourself: read a bit more about these issues. This will give you more confidence to take action. Read books about environmental and climate justice, including *This Changes Everything* and *On Fire: The Burning Case for a Green New Deal* by Naomi Klein and *Merchants of Doubt* by Naomi Oreskes. Watch documentaries that will radicalize you to make change, such as *An Inconvenient Sequel: Truth to Power*, *Chasing Coral*, *Before the Flood*, *A Message from the Future*, and the biopic *Erin Brockovich*.

Connect with trained experts for a personalized look at climate solutions. Attend a presentation (maybe virtually) from a trained leader in climate justice. Learn to answer common questions about the climate crisis. Then, inform others on the basics of climate change and contact relevant decision makers in your area. Write letters to politicians, to newspapers, to companies that are operating in unethical ways (e.g., businesses using palm oil). You could aim to write one letter or email a week.

Become a trusted messenger about climate action in your community and use social media to raise your voice online, inviting others to join the cause.

Participate in a local group with a focus on sustainability. Find a group that shares your priorities. Joining a climate organization helps makes the fight for the planet feel less lonely and more possible. Consider Extinction Rebellion, Sunrise Movement, Climate Reality Project, Zero Hour, Citizens' Climate Lobby, Fridays for Future, and the Sierra Club. Donate to one of the many amazing activist groups working to combat climate change.

Divest from fossil fuels. Ride your bike or walk instead of driving. Pressure your local community to use ethanol-fueled buses for public transportation. If coal is popular in the region where you live, speak up and be vocal about the dangers of coal exhaust.

Grow food. Growing your own food ensures a cheap (read: *free*) healthy meal and a more intimate relationship with the natural processes that produce it. Gardening can be a relaxing activity as well. Many Black communities are food deserts, meaning there is a lack of local produce and adequate healthy, nourishing foods. Find out if there is a community garden in your area and check it out, or see about starting one if there isn't. You could also start composting too, if you really wanted to get crazy.

Organize a virtual strike.

Zeena Abdulkarim is a first-generation Sudanese-American Muslim woman who lives in Atlanta, Georgia. The young activist believes it's important to recognize that social justice and environmental justice go hand in hand. "Minority and low-income communities do not have equal resources and socioeconomic status that ones of greater privilege might [possess], therefore in terms of 'solving' the climate crisis, we must dismantle systems of oppression to ensure that certain communities are not at greater environmental risks than others. This means low-income families, Black and brown communities, women of color, indigenous communities, and other underrepresented and unsupported groups of people."

Affirmations Station

✦ Today, I will spend some time in nature admiring its beauty and nurturing its health.

✦ Today, I will respect Mother Earth by honoring her resources and treading lightly.

✦ Today, I will be thankful for what the land provides to me and honor those who grow the food I eat.

✦ Today, I will nourish seeds, whether they are plants or ideas to make the world a better place.

✦ Today, I will protect all life, whether it is plant, animal, or human, and treat it with care.

✦ Today, I will spend my time or resources on things that have a positive impact on a global scale.

✦ Today, I will focus on the plight of the hungry and envision a full plate for everyone. I will seek out guidance as to how to make my vision an actuality.

Badass to the Bone

"Let us remember our privilege for being here and the work of hundreds of indigenous activists before us. We strike because we can. Because the media focuses on some and not others. But many can't... This movement is not one person, or one group. This movement is all of us and we need to make sure we value those who are disproportionately affected by this crisis."

—**Isra Hirsi**, climate activist and director of the U.S. Youth Climate Strike; after noticing that her school's environmental club wasn't inclusive, she became an advocate for diversity and intersectionality in climate justice

"Your voice can be heard, and even if you're big, small, old, young, it doesn't really matter. You can still make a change in the world."

—**Mari Copeny**, young activist from Flint, MI; after she wrote a letter inviting President Obama to discuss the Flint water crisis, he authorized a budget to fix their water systems

"Most people do not care what they do to the environment. I noticed adults were not willing to offer leadership and I chose to volunteer myself. Environmental injustice is injustice to me."

—**Leah Namugerwa**, climate activist from Uganda; for her fifteenth birthday, she decided to plant two hundred trees in lieu of presents and a party

"I try to make sure that people who have traditionally not been allowed—or included—in places where decisions are made to be in those spaces so they can speak for themselves and influence environmental, public health, and policy issues."

—**Adrienne Hollis**, biomedical scientist and environmental lawyer; she used her time at Florida Agricultural and Mechanical University to help create a toxicology curriculum for communities impacted by environmental racism

"It's a special time where we're building healthy movement. We don't have to sacrifice ourselves in the process. Nobody has to be sacrificed for the world to be better. This mindset that there's not enough for everyone to have something—fuck that. It's white supremacy."

—**Lindsay Harper**, Atlanta-based organizer; the first Black woman to become executive director of Georgia WAND, a women-led advocacy group that works toward ending nuclear proliferation and stemming pollution

"Black folks, low-income folks, and other people of color and indigenous peoples contribute the least to environmental destruction, yet we experience the worst impacts of climate change and pollution."

—**Rachel Stevens**, Los Angeles-based community organizer who has created a space for Black Queer voices to join the fight against fossil fuel usage

"I wanted to study something that would help protect Dominica, and given that climate change is one of our biggest threats, I chose environmental law so we could have access to legal tools in the fight against climate change. Now that I live in the US, I realize that climate change is an issue about inequality—not only between countries, but also between people from different racial and socioeconomic backgrounds."

—**Ama Francis**, environmental lawyer; she advocates for citizens of the Caribbean island of Dominica to have the tools to fight climate change

"Know your true history. We are an agrarian people. We were brought here enslaved not as unskilled labor, but as skilled and knowledgeable farmers… Long ago we were told to leave the land for a better life. Instead, we forgot it's the land that gives us our power. Now we know, as Mother Nature calls us back to where we came from, to once again become stewards of the land."

—**Karen Washington**, farmer and activist; she turned empty lots all throughout New York City into thriving community gardens, helping bring fresh produce to her neighbors

"I get to go all over the country in many different places where people are suffering and dying. I'm here now in Los Angeles, where I spend a lot of my time, and there are families that live a few feet away from oil drilling sites. They look outside their window and see people working in hazmat suits—but these families don't have hazmat suits!"

—**Antonique Smith**, singer, actor, and activist; a Grammy-nominated performer, she has used her platforms to promote environmental justice

"There are many of us young Black environmentalists doing this work. Yet, it feels very lonely at times. We may not be in rooms together, but be assured that your fellow young Black environmentalists are carrying the same messages in spaces that have historically dismissed us. Our voices may shake and our hands may quiver when delivering these truths, but stand strong in your calling. Be brave. Be bold. And be Black."

—**Halston Sleets**, corporate sustainability officer and advocate; she encourages Black people in the environmental justice movement to be bold and loud about their presence and ideas

Fight for Gender Equality

"No person is your friend (or kin) who demands your silence or denies your right to grow and be perceived as fully blossomed as you were intended."

—**Alice Walker**, American novelist, short-story writer, poet, and social activist

When you think about gender equality, what are some of the causes you care about? Some activists work actively to help women identify the insidious impact of patriarchy in everyday life and teach them about equality. Others focus on fighting sexism in higher education; they denounce violence, gender stereotypes, and professional inequalities. As an activist, you may also choose to combat violence against women (including rape, feminicide, and human trafficking) and work on bringing the perpetrators of violence to justice. Violence includes *economic* violence—the precariousness and inequalities that weigh on women because of a capitalist and neo-liberal system which allows male domination to spread and strengthen.

"God, make me so uncomfortable that I will do the very thing I fear."

—**Ruby Dee**, American actress, poet, playwright, screenwriter, journalist, and civil rights activist

"I have come to believe over and over again that what is most important to me must be spoken, made verbal and shared, even at the risk of having it bruised or misunderstood."

—**Audre Lorde**, American author and activist

Fight for LGTBQ+ Rights

LBGTQ+ issues have long been a taboo topic in the Black community. Part of this is due to the strength of the church in the community, and part of it is cultural. But disenfranchising any segment of the population or denying them human rights only leaves us all vulnerable. We should speak out and stand up for those who are targeted and discriminated against. Work to end oppression by supporting and advocating for those who are stigmatized, discriminated against, or treated unfairly.

Here are some ways to support LGBTQ+ rights:

+ **Educate** yourself on current legislation involving the LGBTQ+ community and learn how you can help.

+ **Put an end to bullying.** Confront homophobia or transphobia. Speak up; don't let slurs slide. Do not tolerate hate speech, bigoted "jokes," or homophobic behaviors. You may not change anyone's minds, but you may be making someone else in the room feel a little safer. Visit StopBullying. org to find out what to do to help create a safe environment for LGTBQ+ people.

+ **Help lift voices of people of color.** LGBTQ+ people of color face higher rates of unemployment, violence, and poverty. Understand that people of color in the LGBTQ+ community will have different experiences with discrimination, and support artists, writers, and activists working toward equality for LGBTQ+ people as well as people of color.

+ **Register to vote:** The best way to tell our government how you feel is to vote and support equality. Be sure to update your address if you are registered to vote or sign up if you are not.

+ **Stop anti-LGTBQ+ legislation.** Check out the Human Rights Campaign (HRC) to view resources on state-by-state protections against discrimination, and find out how you can get involved in your own state.

+ **Contact your congressperson and share your thoughts.** Write your state senator or representative; they were elected by you and act on your behalf. Let them know how you feel. Send letters supporting LGBTQ+ equality directly to the White House. Let's keep the upper hand by expressing our opinions with respect and professionalism.

✦ **Shop at businesses that support LGBTQ+ equality.**
And boycott those who support anti-LGBTQ+ legislation or
who have anti-queer policies.

✦ **Watch LGBTQ+ television shows** to increase their ratings.

✦ **Give a little.** Or a lot. Make a donation to your favorite
LGBTQ+ nonprofit.

✦ **Come out as an ally:** Anyone can be an ally, regardless of
their sexual orientation and/or gender identity.

✦ **Volunteer for a gay rights organization.** There are
plenty to choose from, whether you volunteer for a national
organization like HRC or GLAAD or volunteer at your local
P-FLAG chapter, getting involved even just a little is a big
help. Look for local community youth centers geared toward
LGBTQ+ youth and see what you can offer them.

✦ **Listen, learn, and support.**

Affirmations Station

✦ I am at peace with myself.

✦ My Black body emits energy and absorbs energy that is good
for me, energy that loves me and respects me.

✦ I want to be a noble example.

✦ I am fair and treat everyone with respect.

✦ I am the person I think I am.

✦ I don't have to be perfect because perfection is the enemy
of greatness.

Badass to the Bone

"It is not our differences that divide us. It is our inability to recognize, accept, and celebrate those differences."

—**Audre Lorde**, American author and activist

"If I wait for someone else to validate my existence, it will mean that I'm shortchanging myself."

—**Zanele Muholi**, South African visual artist and photographer; she uses art to tell stories about Black lesbian, gay, transgender, and intersex experiences

"All my life, I have maintained that the people of the world can learn to live together in peace if they are not brought up in prejudice."

—**Josephine Baker**, American-born French entertainer, French Resistance agent, and civil rights activist

"I am a trans woman. My sisters are trans women. We are not secrets. We are not shameful. We are worthy of respect, desire, and love."

—**Janet Mock**, American writer, television host, director, producer, and transgender rights activist

"If you don't believe in same-sex marriage, then don't marry someone of the same sex."

—**Wanda Sykes**, American actress and comedian; she boldly came out as gay at a California protest against Proposition 8

"We have to talk about liberating minds, as well as liberating societies."

—**Dr. Angela Davis**, American political activist, philosopher, academic, and author

"I would have rather been punished for asserting myself than become another victim of hatred."

—**CeCe McDonald**, transgender advocate; after surviving a hate crime, she spent nineteen months in jail for defending herself, later going on to become a voice for trans rights

"Life is not so much what you accomplish as what you overcome."

—**Robin Roberts**, television broadcaster; she made waves by coming out as gay while working as an anchor on *Good Morning America*

"At this point in my life, I'd like to live as if only love mattered."

—**Tracy Chapman**, American singer-songwriter; after writing her first song when she was eight, she went on to receive several Grammy nominations and became politically active through her music

"Transwomen supporting and loving each other is a revolutionary act."

—**Laverne Cox**, American actress and LGBTQ+ advocate

"Just knowing you can help somebody out, there's a feeling you can't express."

—**Brittney Griner**, Women's National Basketball Association player; at six foot nine, she was one of the youngest players on the U.S. women's basketball team at the 2012 Olympics

"What people want is very simple: they want an America as good as its promise."

—**Barbara Jordan**, American lawyer, educator, and politician

Other Causes

"Know your worth. You will be told almost daily that you are not good enough. Your intelligence, your experience, your insights, and knowledge will continuously be questioned. You will make people uncomfortable simply by your presence in their space. Once you decide that this is your life's work, do not stop and do not be discouraged."

—**Natalie Mebane**, environmental advocate; she works for the National Children's Campaign, which promotes making children a priority in various social justice movements

There are plenty of other worthwhile causes I could have mentioned, like animal rights, child advocacy, literacy, etc.... Whatever you're passionate about, devoting yourself to a cause you believe in deeply will go a long way toward helping you build a better life and the collective activist community build a better planet. When you have something you love, working to protect it feels natural and is satisfying on a very deep, personal level. You also get to meet other people with the same interests, and that's a bunch of badass.

It's Just the Beginning

I hope by now you have a better understanding of why affirmations are so powerful. In the beginning, we discussed the competing voices in your head, that of the inner critic and that of the wise voice of reason. Learning to shut off the inner critic leads you to all kinds of phenomenal insights and understandings. It's not always easy to silence that voice. Even the most successful women in the world battle "imposter syndrome." It can take years of dedicated practice to learn to put that voice aside and listen with your heart to what reason is dictating to you. This is especially hard in a society where Black girls and Black women are devalued or considered "less than." It's important that you don't take cruel comments to heart and internalize them. There are many complex reasons why society has treated Black girls and women as second-class citizens, none of them valid. Remember to treat yourself as an equal to everyone you meet. You'll know you're getting there when you can feel it in your stature. For now, practice standing tall.

Once you open your heart to the kinder, wiser voice within, and follow up your positive affirmations with positive actions, there's no telling what you can accomplish. At first, the changes you see will be in yourself. You'll feel stronger, more confident, and more willing to act in a productive way, but don't be surprised if you start to see changes radiating out from you once you start putting your energy into the world in a concerted manner. Positive energy is contagious, and others will be drawn to you.

Once change has taken effect within you, and you are acting in positive ways, the changes around you will start to ripple out, and you're likely to see some miracles occur in your world (even if they are minor miracles—a miracle is still a miracle).

Remember, the greatest miracle of all is that you are alive and breathing today. The world will open up to you if you approach it with the best intentions and focus your energy on making it a safer, more just, and more equal place for everyone who lives here with you on this little blue planet.

30 Days of Purpose

Day 1—In what aspects of your life would you like to make changes?

Day 2—Right this second, what four things are you thankful about?

Day 3—What scares you the most?

Day 4—Are you happy in the house and neighborhood you live in? Why or why not? Where would you most like to live? Don't limit yourself—it could be anywhere in the world!

Day 5—In six months, how much progress would you like to have made? A year? Five years? Ten years? What are you doing to achieve these goals? Write a list of the top ten goals you want to achieve within a year. Make a list of anything that is preventing you from reaching those goals, like distractions or things you need to take on to reach them. What in the future worries you the most?

Day 6—Which people in your life are most important to you? How many of the people on your list can you depend on to support you in tough times?

Day 7—What are your personal beliefs? What do you want to accomplish most in life? What do you do that sets you afire? What would make you feel more fulfilled? When do you feel most at peace with yourself?

Day 8—What are the words you use to describe yourself? Are they positive or negative? What ten things do you love most about who you are? Which qualities and talents are you most proud of and require very little effort?

Day 9—What would the perfect day look like to you? What is your dream life? What holds you back from living that dream life you imagine?

Day 10—Over the past year, what have you discovered is true today that wasn't a year ago?

Day 11—What can you start doing today to make your life easier and less complicated?

Day 12—If you could have a talk with anyone, dead or alive, who would it be? Why? Who are your role models? Why?

Day 13—What is your personal definition of the word "happiness"? What would bring more happiness into your life? Now, think about this one—what robs you of joy?

Day 14—What have been your biggest changes over the past five years? If you could talk to yourself from five years ago, what would you tell her?

Day 15—If there was no chance of failure, what would you do? If money was unlimited, what would your ideal life look like? (Where would you choose to live, what career would you pursue, what kind of family would you build?)

Day 16—What did someone do recently to make your day better? How can you make someone else's day better?

Day 17—What life lesson or insight have you gained from a recent challenge? How did going through the darkness and struggle change you into who you are right now?

Day 18—If you knew today was your last day alive, what would you do differently? If you could pick one message you'd want to pass along after you've died, what would it be? How would you like to be remembered?

Day 19—Write a profile of the kind of person you wish to be. Create an avatar for this alternate personality. What are their qualities? Where do they work and live? How do they face difficulties? Write down some ways you can incorporate into your life the qualities that your avatar possesses which you think you don't.

Day 20—Write out five positive affirmations about yourself. Repeat them daily.

Day 21—What memory brings you the most joy and satisfaction?

Day 22—If you could live during another time period, when would you most want to be alive? What kind of life would you have?

Day 23—Set a two-minute timer and write down whatever thoughts flash through your mind.

Day 24—What can you do today to bring you closer to achieving your goals?

Day 25—What in life is most important to you? Why?

Day 26—What can you let go of that's holding you back? (Fears, toxic energy, unhealthy relationships?) What bad habits do you need to quit?

Day 27—Draw or paint a picture of something that makes you happy. You can put it in your journal or hang it in your home to remind you to keep your chin up.

Day 28—In what ways do you neglect yourself? How can you start practicing better self-care starting today?

Day 29—What fills you with energy and makes you feel most alive? When was the last time you had that feeling?

Day 30—Make a list of five things you want to try this year that will force you to step out of your comfort zone.

About the Author

Born in Port-au-Prince, Haiti, M.J. Fievre moved to the United States in 2002. She currently writes from Miami.

M.J.'s publishing career began as a teenager in Haiti. At nineteen years-old, she signed her first book contract with Hachette-Deschamps, in Haiti, for the publication of a Young Adult book titled *La Statuette Maléfique*. Since then, M.J. has authored nine books in French that are widely read in Europe and the French Antilles. In 2013, One Moore Book released M.J.'s first children's book, *I Am Riding*, written in three languages: English, French, and Haitian Creole. In 2015, Beating Windward Press published M.J.'s memoir, *A Sky the Color of Chaos*, about her childhood in Haiti during the brutal regime of Jean-Bertrand Aristide.

M.J. Fievre is the author of *Happy, Okay? Poems about Anxiety, Depression, Hope, and Survival* (Books & Books Press, 2019) and *Badass Black Girl: Questions, Quotes, and Affirmations for Teens* (Mango Publishing, 2020). She helps others write their way through trauma, build community and create social change. She works with veterans, disenfranchised youth, cancer patients and survivors, victims of domestic and sexual violence, minorities, the elderly, those with chronic illness or going through transition and any underserved population in need of writing as a form of therapy—even if they don't realize that they need writing or therapy.

A long-time educator and frequent keynote speaker (Tufts University, Massachusetts; Howard University, Washington, D.C.; the University of Miami, Florida; and Michael College, Vermont; and a panelist at the Association of Writers & Writing Programs Conference, AWP), M.J. is available for book club meetings, podcast presentations, interviews and other author events.

Mango Publishing, established in 2014, publishes an eclectic list of books by diverse authors—both new and established voices—on topics ranging from business, personal growth, women's empowerment, LGBTQ studies, health, and spirituality to history, popular culture, time management, decluttering, lifestyle, mental wellness, aging, and sustainable living. We were recently named 2019 *and* 2020's #1 fastest-growing independent publisher by *Publishers Weekly*. Our success is driven by our main goal, which is to publish high-quality books that will entertain readers as well as make a positive difference in their lives.

Our readers are our most important resource; we value your input, suggestions, and ideas. We'd love to hear from you—after all, we are publishing books for you!

Please stay in touch with us and follow us at:

Facebook: Mango Publishing
Twitter: @MangoPublishing
Instagram: @MangoPublishing
LinkedIn: Mango Publishing
Pinterest: Mango Publishing
Newsletter: MangoPublishingGroup.com/newsletter

Join us on Mango's journey to reinvent publishing, one book at a time.